YOUNG FOR YOUR OWN GOOD

Sherry Ellesson

BALBOA.
PRESS

A DIVISION OF HAY HOUSE

Balboa Press books may be ordered through booksellers or by contacting:

Balboa Press
A Division of Hay House
1663 Liberty Drive
Bloomington, IN 47403
www.balboapress.com
1 (877) 407-4847

Because of the dynamic nature of the Internet, any web addresses or
links contained in this book may have changed since publication and
may no longer be valid. The views expressed in this work are solely those
of the author and do not necessarily reflect the views of the publisher,
and the publisher hereby disclaims any responsibility for them.

The author of this book does not dispense medical advice or prescribe the use
of any technique as a form of treatment for physical, emotional, or medical
problems without the advice of a physician, either directly or indirectly. The
intent of the author is only to offer information of a general nature to help
you in your quest for emotional and spiritual well-being. In the event you use
any of the information in this book for yourself, which is your constitutional
right, the author and the publisher assume no responsibility for your actions.

Any people depicted in stock imagery provided by Thinkstock are models,
and such images are being used for illustrative purposes only.
Certain stock imagery © Thinkstock.

Printed in the United States of America.

ISBN: 978-1-4525-9692-1 (sc)
ISBN: 978-1-4525-9693-8 (e)

Balboa Press rev. date: 5/13/2014

CONTENTS

For Big Bird, who has believed in me even when I've doubted myself.

PREFACE

The idea for this book first hatched on my 44th birthday. I had stopped at a liquor store to get some bubbly ...and got carded. Later that day, while the guys were out back making their version of barbecue, their wives and I celebrated what we called the Sherry Ellesson Cheap Champaign on the Front Porch Invitational, and I related the story of the liquor store drama. I did my best to pantomime the look on the clerk's face as, even with the typical, unflattering mug shot staring out at him from my driver's license, he looked suspicious and asked if I had any other kinds of identification with me. My friends laughed, but then one of them paused for a second and, pointing out that even my hands and feet didn't look to her like they belonged on a mature woman, said "Girl, whatever you're doing, you should either bottle it or write a book!"

Fast forward more than fifteen years from that day, to another birthday – my 60th. My gentleman friend and I settled ourselves into our seats at a nice Italian restaurant and I ordered a glass of wine. As we chatted amiably, our server approached and told me she'd need to see some I.D. My thoughts immediately flew to the prospect that there were some sort of escaped convict on the loose and that perhaps I looked like her. Visions of my face on the wall of the Post Office flashed across my mind until she said apologetically, "I believe you're over 21 but the bartender said he has to make sure...."

We stand at a crossroads in human experience, where on the one more traveled avenue, medical science with its devices and chemistry is making it possible to extend what we used to think of as typical life expectancy, albeit, in bodies and minds that come to cry out for the relief of death; while in the crosswise direction, glimpses of the kind of long lives told of in legend and scripture shine so brightly that we are afraid to even look too long in that direction - lives filled with miraculous energy, vitality and youth spanning generations. As though avoiding staring into the sun, we believe we will be damaged if we dare spend too much time considering such possibilities. We dismiss them as perhaps long lost historical tales, the likes of which we will never see again. Do you wonder, as I do, why not? It begs the question:

Were people two, three or more millennia ago privileged in ways we have sacrificed for some egregious violation? We feel as though we've come a long way; and while we're not perfect, haven't we advanced the causes of right living wherever we could? Don't the practices of things like clean living, kindness, and charity toward others count for something? Well, okay then – maybe it's easier to explain the disappearance of these legendary lifetimes as their having been metaphors. Yes, that's it – we didn't mess up. The truth is, people didn't *actually* ever live for hundreds of years - those stories were *metaphors*. Damn. But wait a second here. Are we sure? Can it be proven? Let's suspend disbelief for *just* a moment, and explore a few new ideas that are down that crosswise road.

What if the actuarial tables are only telling part of the story, in their innocent ignorance of what to measure? What if the phrase "correlation is not causation" were never more true than when it comes to our passage through what we *call* time (more on this later, too) and experience? Jump into an ideal future:

What if the term, "mature" were to become a concept twenty-somethings *aspired* to, because they were raised knowing it meant more understanding and personal power than they could ever gain without decade after decade of experience and learning? And while we're at it -- how about some *un*-learning for baby boomers in the meantime?

Part of the wonder of this crossroads right now is that hard core science is shaking hands with ancient spiritual traditions, *and the two are startled to find themselves in agreement.* After all, if we are not against something, aren't we betraying what we're for? Don't the two sets of beliefs comprise an either/or that demands we take sides? They couldn't be saying the same thing, approached from two different perspectives and just using different terminology, could they?

...could they?!

To wrap our minds around this, we're going to have to essentially jettison some of the rules that have defined our personal and cultural paradigms, the biggest being that we actually live in that either/or world. Phrases like, "you're either for me or against me," "you can be right or you can be happy," and my personal favorite, "do it (my version of) right or don't do it at all" define much of our world view. The world is not either A or B but A plus B and a whole hell of a lot more!

We're going to be doing a number spelunking exercises into our own mind-sets, and I can almost guarantee that what will start out feeling a bit stilted will get to be a near-constant stream of ah-ha's as you find yourself dragging a piece of paper out of your pocket or purse, or asking for another paper napkin to write on at the damnedest times. Your mind is holding back an enormous amount of self-awareness that can serve you, behind a pair of what I hope for you will be rather fragile gates, and you have the key. Better yet, just lean against them!

To give you a glimpse of where we're going with this, consider for a moment the ancient Yin & Yang symbol. It is black and white, black and red, or any two distinctly different colors depending on the source, but there's a major truth inside it. The two "opposing" colors do not line up exactly in that "either/or" linear fashion, do they? No, they're curved, each sort of "pushing" the other in that circular motion. Stay with me here, because this is important — there is also a smaller circle within each of the two color fields containing some of its opposite.

Look at the word, "opposite" and its root word, "oppose." But are the two parts of the symbol really opposing each other? Or are they instead actually driving a push/pull, rhythmic sharing that is the energy that perpetuates life? Hmm.... Okay, so some folks reading this feel very uncomfortable right now. I get it. We laugh at the idea of thought police; but at the same time, thinking outside even our own mental box is a little weird. It is so much easier to think in terms of black and white, right and wrong, what works and what doesn't, and most of the people we spend our time with are operating under the same constraints and will back us up as long as we think this way. But look at our lives as they really function and consider an equally popular phrase, "it's complicated."

We know, whether we like it or not, that we don't typically operate in a clear, right-angled world. In point of fact, we ebb and flow, and the most creative and beautiful parts of life on this gorgeous orb of ours include infinite variety of thought and choice, and things that don't fit neatly into either/or... and that, my friends, is very freeing. Scary sometimes, but freeing.

This book is about finding freedom by escaping the early 21st century's current perceptions of limitation around the subject of aging. Yes, we will discuss the things that immediately leap to mind, such as diet and exercise because they have an important place in this work. We'll also talk about what used to be called "airy-fairy" things like alternative, non-invasive therapies that have gone pretty much mainstream, and we'll see that all forms of healing can work in concert. Eventually though, we'll bring it full circle, just like that Yin/Yang symbol, and do the important work of finding the drivers – the deepest beliefs that comprise our personal paradigms, and learn how to expand and educate them until they eventually bend to our will for the highest good of each of us, *because we want it.*

Along the way, we will also (yes, go ahead and cringe now and get it over with) talk *in layman's terms* about things like quantum physics and epigenetics (I did mention hard-core science, remember) and how we can use even a surface-level understanding of them to stop being passive bystanders in the creation of our lives and take the conscious, deliberate reins of what we call aging.

INTRODUCTION

At one time in recorded human history, the known world in Europe consisted of Europe, and anything outside its immediate oceanic borders was believed to be off the edge of this flat disk called Earth, roiling with monsters waiting to grasp and digest any who ventured too far from the familiar. The best science of the day held to this view and for all intents and purposes it was "true." But it wasn't, was it.

Fast forward to an accidental discovery in 1895, when the use of X-Rays enabled people to look inside the human body for the first time without cutting it open. Up to that point, the only way of viewing a break in a bone or a swallowed object was to incise. The best medical science of the day held to this view and for all intents and purposes it was "true." But it wasn't, was it.

Another step forward a few years just prior to November of 1903, when the notion of a self-powered and controlled vehicle that could travel through the air was impossible. The best science of the day held to this view and for all intents and purposes it was "true." ...you know the rest.

We live in a world of accelerating discovery, and in spite of having seen astonishing advances measured now not in centuries but in *months*, we stubbornly cling to some old beliefs – old entire systems of *assumptions* that limit us. We believe, for instance, that "the only things we can be sure of are death and taxes." We believe, "none of us is getting any younger." We believe, "you can't turn back the clock." Are we sure? Could it be that the best science of the day right now is discovering that these too are mistaken beliefs born of assigning causation to what is merely correlation? Are we operating under old rules of belief based on a science that has been supplanted with new discoveries?

I have a running joke with some friends, that every time I go to the pet supply store for dog food or cat food, it rains. It happened maybe twice or three times in a few months some years back; and now, whenever it hasn't rained for a while and gardens are begging for water, my friends will ask, "don't you need something from the pet supply?" Obviously, they're kidding - it would seem ridiculous to us for someone to claim that there absolutely is a cause-and-effect relationship between my buying dog food and the onset of a downpour, but suppose my friends repeated the tale to their friends and families, and those folks in turn repeated it over the course of a couple of generations. How long do you suppose it would it take before this became a superstition? And isn't superstition just a belief in the making?

Don't the oft' repeated sayings eventually plant themselves in our psyches to a point where we repeat them ourselves without thinking? More importantly - without judging or filtering them for truth? A lot of research has been done on the phenomenon of thought being "programmed" just like a computer, and then affecting everything from our choices and behavior to the way our bodies perform in athletic pursuit. Athletes visualize success and go on to achieve it. It becomes part of their cellular memory through repetition of thought pictures; and even when incapacitated for a time, they deliberately affect how their bodies will handle the challenges of their sport as soon as they're up and back into it. And what of this modality for healing? Ever heard of the placebo effect?

All the placebo effect is, is the ability of the mind to affect healing, independent of medical intervention. Mind over matter (although quantum "entanglement" tells us they are nowhere near separate entities). Everything from cancer going into remission to the reassembly of broken bodies has been recorded using a "placebo" of some kind, whether in the form of a sugar pill or the laying on of a faith healer's hands. The mind that's in charge of the body being healed is at the core of this effect, and it can be trained and retrained to change what we've come to accept as limitation, and I think it's about time we learned how to do that. All of us – not just the exceptional athlete or the trained energy-worker.

Why should we accept any oft' repeated precept? Just because it's been repeated often? Or because nobody has yet disproven it? Isn't that what it usually takes to tip social consciousness over the edge? Think about this. All it takes is one person to accomplish something - to step past a previously accepted limitation - for the rest of humanity to realize that it as a species is not limited in that way. One surgeon transplanted a human heart and we knew it could be done. One runner broke the four-minute mile and it became doable. OK...I'll give you this one - it took two Wright brothers to fly, but one flight did it, and from then on, we knew that as a worldwide population we were no longer limited to hot-air balloons to see the ground from a bird's altitude. That's all it takes. One person stepping past a long-held limit. Just once.

So, what's keeping you from turning back the clock? What's keeping any of us from getting any younger? Why is death inevitable? Note here, with tongue planted firmly in cheek, that I don't take on the subject of taxes, as I think there may well be some immutable cosmic rule going on there, so I'm not going to challenge it just yet. But I do think that where individual human potential is concerned, we've been short-changing ourselves for long enough, and I can't think of a better place to start than with this idea of aging, and especially aging involving sickness, frailty, inevitable incapacity...ugh! who needs it?!

Thinking the way others have taught us to think is easy. Not pleasant, maybe - especially where the subject of aging as we've come to accept it is concerned - but definitely easier than changing the way we think. But let me ask you something: is changing your life worth changing your mind? If you knew beyond a shadow of a doubt that changing your internal programming could change how or even whether or not you'd age, would you consider doing it? Would it be worth the discomfort of overcoming years of mental inertia?

Right now, make no mistake - there is a shadow of a doubt. But that's all it is - a shadow. It's habitual thought which has over generations become a belief. Belief has become how our bodies work, and *that belief is running the show.* If an athlete who's laid up with broken bones keeps visualizing skiing down a mountain, and months later goes on to race successfully in the Olympics, why can't we visualize our bodies shrugging off the confines of old programming and rejuvenating themselves *as our cellular structures naturally tend to do?* Why indeed.

This book is about taking a trip - a journey both deeper within than we might have been willing to go before, and a series of steps forward to a place outside currently accepted limitation. I say it's a series of steps because, while I believe that quantum leaps are indeed not only possible but happen every day, they're not the way most of us are conditioned to operate. If we're going to make big changes, we fare better making small steps, in a specific order. We may believe in the idea of life-changing enlightenment but we don't expect it for ourselves. It's not part of our own paradigm. We want a clear road map with mile markers.

We need to be able to look back over our shoulders at any time and see that we've made progress. We crave a certain amount of what's been meanly labeled "immediate gratification" (as though that were a *bad* thing!) if we're to stay the course. For folks with the biggest changes to make, and I'll talk more about this later, this can be a lonely journey. It can feel as though it's us as individuals against the world; and for every one true friend who says, "wow... maybe...hey, what if...?" there will be a crowd who will say, "You're deluding yourself. That's impossible," and you have to be prepared to say to them, "Yeah, right." Just like space flight was impossible. Just like the quantum physicists who have documented particles existing in two places at the same time are deluding themselves.

We'll need to develop the ability to look within at times like that, listen to our gut instead of the naysayers, and find the strength not to argue our point or justify our belief in ourselves, but to quietly and determinedly move toward what we want. Yes, I believe we'll prove them wrong. And we'll try our best not to be smug...won't we?

So...are you ready? Are you willing to find that what you believed was a "can't do" is just a "didn't do before"? Would it feel wonderful to look back in 30 days, 90 days, a year from now...best yet, a full 7 years from now (which we're told is how long the slowest-regenerating bodily tissues take to rebuild) and see that what you thought was a barrier has easily and gently been surpassed? That last idea there is one that's tough for most people to accept - that breaking through any barrier can be easy. But I'm here to say it can be, and the way to do it is to be willing to look at the trees instead of the whole forest. That's not to say, don't keep your eye on the goal. Do, absolutely.

What it means is, be willing to take the journey step by incremental step - sometimes a baby step, sometimes a stretch. Baby steps will consist of actual physical habits that you can and probably will need to change to clear the way for your new way of experiencing your life. Stretches will come in the mental and emotional arena, where you'll have some new ideas to try on - ideas that may at times seem esoteric at best and at their weirdest, more "airy-fairy" than your logical self wants to fool around with. But if you stay with it -- suspend *dis*belief for a while -- and keep trying on the new ideas and ways of doing things until they're less uncomfortable, you will indeed be looking over your shoulder before long and feeling quite differently.

Ready?

Good. You are not alone in this. I'm here and so is everyone else who's tired of this false limit.

Turn the page.

CHAPTER 1

What Were You Thinking?! or
Who's Doing Your Thinking?

Most of us believe we think for ourselves. We point to our jobs, where we live, whether or not we have pets, and which bank we go to as evidence of our freedom of choice. We talk about our food preferences, the kind of things we like to keep on our desks, and where we most like to go if we get some time off. Those are the larger, more tangible kinds of evidence of choice, and we don't much question any of our thought processes beyond those. But stop and consider for a moment how much we do, say, and in many cases actually *believe*, based on what are actually pre-chosen patterns running like a computer program out of sight, out of *conscious* mind. How many phrases, actions and even relationships do we repeat, without ever asking ourselves why?

One of the words that have become ubiquitous, at least in Western culture, has been the word "choice." We hear from people in the news making tearful confessions, "I made bad choices," or we read in advice columns, "you made this choice…." and we assume that yes, we are choosers. But who's really doing the choosing? Is the surface, aware self – the one who looks around in the cafeteria and finds a seat, or the one who looks at wallpaper samples and decides on texture over print – the one who's doing our choosing? Or could it be that there's something silent and insidious going on behind the scenes that actually runs the vastly greater proportion of our lives….and we let it?

Stop and think for a minute about your breathing. If you exercise on a regular basis or practice Yoga, you've probably given some consideration to your breathing, at least during those times when you're actively participating in those pursuits. But what about the rest of the time? Who's choosing to inhale and exhale? Who's deciding to make your heart beat? Who chooses to blink your eyes or make you yawn? Of course, we take these functions for granted, and blithely murmur, "that's just the way the body works." Yes, it is, but it's not without a thousand decisions – choices – going on in every moment. The chooser is what many call the "subconscious," and it is the much bigger, *much more powerful* part of each of our minds – and folks, in large measure, it's running us.

It is our personal super-computer, and it operates at such a speed and volume of information exchange that the conscious mind would burn out and exhaust itself if it tried to do even a fraction of what the subconscious does. So that's the good news. We've got a hell of an operating system going for us and all we have to do is trust that the programming works, and all will be well. Ah, but there's the rub. All isn't always well, and because we're so sure we're choosing, we don't stop and ask ourselves an important set of questions when it feels like things are going wrong: what exactly is this program we've got going? Who fed it into the computer? And if something's going wrong, who does the debugging?

We don't ask ourselves these questions because we think we already know the answers (hint: they're part of the programming too) and we don't question them, even when what's happening with our health, our relationships, or our jobs isn't going the way we're sure we would choose. The answers we typically come up with are things like, "this (health issue) runs in my family," or "this always happens to me – I have the worst luck," or "I didn't have the advantages s/he did" and we pretty much doom ourselves to the feelings of powerlessness that go with all of those. Going back to the computer analogy, let's look at what a program for bad relationships might look like:

>Let you be Person A

>Let potential partner be Person B

>Let bad behavior be XYZ

>Start

1> Person A recognizes not XYZ in Person B for 3 months

2> If Person B does XYZ then go to End

3> Else if Person B does not XYZ continue 1 month

4> Go to 2>

>End

Note in the above program, there is no allowance for the relationship to ever get past step 2 for very long. A person with this kind of programming may not even realize they believe at a very deep, hidden level that relationships last a few precious months and then inevitably disintegrate because of a predictable behavior on the other person's part. Does this sound farfetched? Or do you recognize this in someone you know? Don't most of us know at least one somebody who consistently picks "the wrong" wo/man and goes through the same three-act play over and over again? What if I were to tell you that the same kind of patterns – programs – run whole segments of all our lives, and that we need to become aware of the fact that they're there, if we ever want to be able to break free of the ones that don't work?

Try this little experiment for yourself: Hold your dominant hand up in front of your face, a little to the side, and make a talking gesture with your fingers, as though you were signaling to someone across the room that whoever is on the phone won't stop talking. Got that? OK...keep doing the quack quack gesture as you slowly pull your hand back, along the side of your face and then toward the back of your head. Can you still see your hand moving? At some point, usually right around the level of your ear, most people's peripheral vision will check out and the "talking" is going on unseen. It's still back there making noise and carrying on though, and while it may be out of sight, out of (conscious) mind, it's *still back there running its mouth.*

If the talking it's doing is endlessly saying, "I'll always have a weight problem," or "nobody in my family ever has any money" or "I never did anything to deserve...<fill in the blank>" then unless the conscious mind decides to climb in the back seat and figure out a way to change the program, it keeps running in an endless loop. And guess whose life doesn't feel very good in that particular area. So, okay then – all this talk of programming is well and good, and most psychologists will back up the idea that a huge amount of what we believe just happens to us is actually preprogrammed, then the next question goes back to those original ones I asked you to consider earlier: what's the program I'm carrying out and how did it get in my head? I'm glad you asked.

Back in what we now think of as the Dark Ages of the discipline of psychology, some pretty bright people found that most kids don't even develop this "filter" called the conscious mind until around the age of 6. They found that in the earliest years, the subconscious (that super-computer, though they didn't have that analogy to draw on) is wide open, totally unquestioning, accepting everything and anything that was seen, heard, *and felt* from its mother, other caretakers, people the caretakers interacted with, the environment – all of it - whether it was intended as input for the child or not.

5

Some psychologists believe that this input actually begins before the moment of birth, while the fetus is still *in utero*. Stop and think about what's going into that developing mind – the wide open one that's accepting everything. What went into yours? Were your mother and father insanely grateful that they were expecting a child, or were you "a surprise"? Did Mom have some postpartum depression to deal with? Did you have older sibs who were either glad you came into the world or maybe not so much? Most of us get a mixed bag right from the start, and it doesn't stop there.

I was raised by my grandparents, after being bounced between foster homes for a few years until age 4. My grandfather did not want to raise another child, and certainly not a girl. My grandmother, on the other hand, saw "an angel" that she hadn't had to carry through pregnancy, and she loved children, so I became theirs. My dad was far too young to be expected to assume any childrearing responsibilities, and was more than happy to leave me in their care. He'd stay with them between girlfriends, pay attention to me when it would impress the latest girl if she liked kids, and then disappear again. What kind of messages did the child mind that was me get?

I remember some things my grandparents did say that were very empowering, such as, "you can do anything you put your mind to," and "what a smart girl!" I got my first microscope at age six, and winters between ages eight and fourteen were punctuated with climbing out onto the porch roof with telescopes and looking at the stars. The neighbors who saw us out on the roof probably thought we had all snapped, but that's a whole different story. The message often during those years was that there were boundless worlds that not everyone tuned in to that were amazing and important, and I still believe that.

I also recall some programming that ran crosswise to those self-same messages. "Girls aren't good at math," meant that in the accelerated division in junior high, I took Latin, composition and science with the really smart kids and math with those for whom the subject was a stumbling block.

Imagine how weird it felt when I got my first A in math in Mr Poli's Geometry class. It got even weirder when as an adult, I was designing my house and realized I was easily using a formula from an Algebra class I had struggled with, to figure out how high above the ground the peak of the roof would be, given a certain rise-to-run roof pitch. I wasn't carrying out the "girls aren't good in Math" program anymore because I had changed it years before, out of necessity for my job.

Here's another exercise – and this one may surprise you if you can relax with it and let the ideas flow: get out another piece of paper and start writing down time-worn phrases about any particular subject (money, social status – you pick) that you used to hear around your house as you were growing up. The person(s) you heard them from isn't important right now – good or not-so-good, start writing. Most people begin slowly and once those floodgates open, they can hardly write fast enough. Use several pages if you have to, until you feel as though you've dumped a lot out onto the paper, and don't be surprised if you get a serious emotional reaction when you do this.

My friend Ellie came from a family whose portrait is probably right next to the word Accomplishment in the dictionary. She heard me talking to a group of people one day about early-childhood programming and at first, she didn't want to do the exercise because clearly, her family's messages must have been very strong and affirming or they wouldn't have been as successful as they were. Nonetheless, she had often found that she herself would go only so high in whatever company she did human resources work for, before hitting the proverbial "glass ceiling." She pointed to other women who had experienced similar limitations and deemed the whole thing a result of the "good ole boy network" but it troubled her, so she began her list.

I noticed that it took her a few minutes to come up with the first line; but after a while, she was writing so fast and with such energy I didn't immediately notice the tears streaming down her face. She was one of the last to finish, her face flushed and her mascara leaving black streaks down her cheeks. She didn't wait for the end of the class, but left the room.

She shared with me later that she had phoned her mother and startled her with some rather penetrating questions – why was Daddy's job "the real one" and yours was just for extra money? You didn't even like that job - why didn't you quit and find something you enjoyed? Why didn't you play tennis anymore after you and Daddy got married? You even had trophies you won.... And on it went, until Ellie realized that in her mother's efforts to be the supportive, self-sacrificing wife she believed she should be – *that she herself had been programmed to be* - she had passed on a paradigm of built-in professional defeat and lack of self-fulfillment to her daughter. And this last is something to remember.

Ellie's mother didn't deliberately hold her daughter back or inculcate her with unhappiness – she was just carrying out the patterns *she* had been taught, totally *un*consciously, and it's entirely possible that if Ellie hadn't been in that classroom that day, she might have done exactly the same thing to/for any daughter she might have had. Ellie's story and her mother's before her are hardly a worst-case scenario.

All day every day, people pass on to their kids the same inner monologues they've been living themselves, often based not on choice, but on what they've seen and heard repeatedly since infancy themselves and gone on to believe and gone on to live - self-fulfilling prophecies. And let's keep in mind, not all stories are even somewhat affirming, as Ellie's was.

What of the impoverished mother who bemoans the lack of a present and responsible father for her children. What do her daughters come to expect when they hear, "that's the way men are…they use you and run out on you." What does the boy brought into the world of a family with chronic illness grow up believing about his physical self when he sees his mother bedridden, or his older sister demonstrating silent resentment at having to care for the ailing parent.

He can't win. If he's sick, somebody hates taking care of him; and if he's not sick, he may end up doing the caregiving and hating it. The concept of health being the more natural state of the human body is foreign to him, or perhaps he believes it's only "for other people."

What this all comes down to is that in pretty much every area of our lives, the people we spent our earliest years with passed on programming that they got from people who got it from their early upbringing and so on. That programming becomes a series of instructions that we "believe" and we go on to live out the programming, further reinforcing it. It affects our health, our relationships, our ability to earn money, our self-images, and our beliefs about pretty much everything. It becomes our personal paradigm.

Bringing this back to the subject of aging, what can *any* of us do, when we've heard from early childhood and through most of our adult years (as though it needed reinforcement) that X number of years is about the most we can expect to live? How many times have we heard, "well, he was 90, so he lived a good long life," or "I guess we should have been ready for this…after all, she's in her 80s…."

This leads me to yet another exercise, which can actually get to be kind of fun when you think about it – get out more paper and make a list of age-related phrases you heard/hear/ sometimes repeat. Really – do this, because the more aware you are of the things you see, hear, and through repetition have come to *believe*, the better. Awareness is power.

People over the age of 40 often bemoan the fact that "we live in an age-obsessed culture" and at the same time, we continue to think, feel, speak and at some level *fear* a near-constant stream of messages about aging, without the slightest notion of what it's doing to our own physiology – how we're affecting or reinforcing the programming of that super-computer that's running the show. Now, I'll grant you, it could look at this point as though we're pretty much stuck with whatever programs we've been fed – good, bad or a mix of – from earliest childhood, with a word from our sponsor (genetics) thrown in, but there's good news, and... more good news.

We are not cast in a hard shell of thought with a tempered glass neuro-net that cannot be reshaped. Let me say that a different way – if we consider that the thoughts we think actually affect the physical synapses in the brain forming "relationships," if you will, then the door is left open to change those relationships. If I associate aging with freedom from being at the mercy of others' opinions, with having time for creativity that I didn't have during childbearing years, with developing my own personal style rather than being a slave to trends, do you see where practicing these thoughts might throw a whole new complexion on maturing?

Paradigms and assumptions can die hard – especially when we see so much "correlation" that everyone around us is assuming is "causation" - but they can and *must* be changed if we're ever to break out of old patterns and find the wonderful new ones that other branches of science and technology have breached and conquered. There would appear to be two different ways to approach the challenge, i.e. from the standpoint of the scientific or that of the spiritual, but there is already, as John Polkinghorne calls it, an "unexpected kinship" developing between the two. We get to throw out the either/or and find what works within each of us as we look to how we *feel* and get to know ourselves at depth.

CHAPTER 2

DNA, RNA, Who Are These Guys Anyway? (rah! rah! rah!)

One of the culprits most often blamed for the rate, condition and surrounding "symptoms" of aging (as though it were a disease) is Genetics. We all studied the double helix in science class as kids, and some people have gone on to make it their life's work. We're told there is a blueprint that's passed on from one generation to the next and (depending on whom you talk to) it controls anywhere from a little to a lot of how our bodies function (or don't, past a certain point.) We credit our genes with eye color and hair texture and blame them unmercifully for everything from our overly round waistlines to a tendency toward allergies, alcoholism and everything else beginning with A...through Z.

I'll share with you here that back when I believed I might be a "victim" of some of my genetic makeup, I briefly entertained a niggling fear that I didn't want to look at; namely, that nobody on either side of my family had lived to a "ripe old age." In my old paradigm, "we" were a family of relatively short-lived folks. But there was a contradiction somewhere in my psyche, and while I can't identify where it came from, I live in gratitude for it every day.

I think I noticed it probably when I was somewhere around eight or nine years old. My great aunt, who was a lovable obese woman, often sighed wistfully about her size (as she put away a plateful of graham crackers and peanut butter) and she'd admonish me, "when you get to be my age, you'll see...." The implication of course was that whatever she felt went with her age – the extra weight, the difficulty moving around, the large-sized clothes that never looked right -- were to be my fate as well past a certain age, whatever that was.

She would talk endlessly about the latest diet, and while I never did see her trim down, I suspect she did at times lose a few pounds and then put them back on. Her wedding picture described a much thinner woman with some pretty curves; but her programming clearly put her in a different body past that certain age. Here's the part I call the contradiction: I looked at her one day, and without a shred of either meanness or sympathy, thought to myself, "I'm *not* going to be like you when I get older." Somewhere in that stroke of defiant intention, the "we" of my family stopped including me, at least where that particular part of the blueprint got activated.

Somehow, perhaps during the discussions my family had over the coffee table loaded with Adele Davis' books on Nutrition and Norman Vincent Peale's on positive thinking,

I had gotten the crazy notion that I could be different from my family if I wanted to, and I wanted to. Now, that said, I've become aware as I've studied and done research, that I undoubtedly still did take in a lot of crappy programming that stuck for too many years; but I find, as I hope you will should you pursue this, that even stubborn old ideas and beliefs can be changed, released or reworked, and *it's worth the effort*. We're talking about affecting how your genetic blueprint works here – and you have more control than you think.

There are two resources I'd like for you to write down, now that you've filled up some pages with things I hope have been eye-openers. One is a book written by Dr Bruce Lipton titled *The Biology of Belief*, and the other is a film called *What the Bleep Do We Know?* (which actually features Dr Lipton along with Dr Candace Pert and numerous other scientists). For me, watching the film first, with its wonderful, humorous animation of cells reacting to brain chemicals and then reading Dr Lipton's book, which gave an even more scientific but still very understandable explanation of why/ how those chemicals affect our DNA, were like blinding flashes of light.

I won't spoil the film or the book for you, but an important insight I got from them is that, depending upon what thoughts I continue to think (whether I'm aware of them or not – remember that subconscious talk that's always going on) and the brain chemistry they prompt, my cells are ordered to carry out some parts of the genetic blueprint

I carry around, while others may never see the light of day, so to speak. Think about that.

If a certain image deeply embedded in my neuro-net (electro-chemical pathways) makes me afraid when I consider/remember/regard something, the part of my brain known as the Hypothalamus spews out corresponding fear-related peptides. My entire body is flooded with fear chemicals, and goes into all the various kinds of states related to fear. Now, a little fear can be a good thing – especially when you need to run very fast away from a ticked off dog, lift a car off your kid or perform some other superhuman feat for survival. But too much, too often gets exhausting and it's bad for your cells. They can't keep up, constantly trying to slough off the toxic byproducts of that extreme, without suffering some damage, and the parts of your DNA that could enable you to write a symphony, paint in the Impressionist style or spread healing, loving *rejuvenating* energy through your own body may never get a chance to function the way the cells and organ systems are designed to do.

We'll talk more later in this book about the importance of elimination of toxins from the body (you knew we'd get around to it, didn't you?) but for right now, the message I want you to absorb is that thoughts – whether they're the conscious kind that you *choose* to spend air time on or the subconscious kind we've been calling programming – are affecting your brain's generation of what are called "psycho-pharmaceuticals," and those chemicals are affecting how your body looks, feels and functions in every moment. The cells are deciding, based on the chemicals surrounding them and interacting with them, what parts of your DNA get activated and which remain unused. Premature aging, anyone?

So, you may ask, if we can get into the habit of trying to skew our conscious (deliberately chosen) thoughts to the good side, with things like meditation, affirmations, keeping reminders of happy times around and so on, that sounds like a pretty good thing; but what about those other thoughts – the subconscious ones that are bigger, faster and way more powerful? Can those be changed? And if so, *how?* I said I had good news and good news.

The first good news is yes, those old programs can be changed; and the how of it is a wide, wonderful world that can involve various do-it-yourself techniques, like self-hypnosis, subliminals and paraliminals, the use of what are called binaural beats, visualization – even some of the same things that work on the conscious mind, provided they're done often enough, deliberately, and with focus. Keep in mind that learning to drive a car starts off taking 100% of our focus and must be practiced; but at some point, we can get into our cars, have an intention of where we want to end up, and the trip from point A to point B often is driven on autopilot.

There are lots of things the average, everyday person can do, and we'll talk about some of them before we're done. One of the simplest and most powerful first steps, however, is to become *aware* of those non-useful programs, and prepare for the fact that the spelunking and overwriting can take time and much repetition. The other good news is that the reprogramming involves imagining, playing games, making fun lists, and allowing ourselves to feel the beauty and happiness that wells up inside when we truly allow ourselves to dream and eventually to believe.

The practice part is not arduous or painful – indeed, it involves selectively *choosing focus* on all that is wanted and good. We don't have to extract the old programs or make any effort about them at all once they're identified; in fact, the less airtime we give them the better – they'll atrophy all by themselves as we introduce, play and replay imagery and emotions that feel so much better.

At this point, I'd like to make a strong recommendation for a book by Esther and Jerry Hicks called *Ask and It Is Given*. That sounds as though it would be a religious treatise, and while there are references to scripture of various kinds quoted occasionally to make a point, the book has a whole section beginning with Part II where there are a series of "processes" that can be used to incrementally climb the emotional scale. They're fun stuff – games, if you will - and their value is in being able to start anywhere, from feeling helpless and in despair all the way up to blissed out and wanting more, and being able to practice the good feelings until they become the preponderance of how we experience our day to day lives. It's what Abraham calls climbing the emotional scale, and I can attest to its power to change lives. Thoughts have been compared to the structure of our rocket, while the feelings that arise from them are the fuel.

One analogy I've drawn myself and seen in other sources is that of the human psyche being much like an onion. As we start making the conscious effort to learn more about what's under our everyday habits and language around what we like, don't like, and believe - when we start observing our own patterns and especially our reactions, we unwrap what is often a surprising package with multiple layers. Some of them turn out to be delightful, while some are difficult and even painful to look at and allow. But allow we must, as no human being is all sweetness and light – that side that we might term "dark" or "angry" or "hurt" has to be allowed to make itself known to us, as these reactions are the key to what may be holding us back the most.

I don't think any of us wants to spend a lot of time in a dark place; but we need to know it's there within each of us and *let that be okay*. It is not a fatal flaw – it's just part of that whole self we're unwrapping and getting to know. We get to choose – consciously, from a place of heightened awareness – which parts we cultivate and which we allow to rest or fade away entirely. The relationships within the brain between the way the synapses arrange themselves is a bit like casual personal relationships with people we see in our workplace, the supermarket – anyplace we frequent. If we pay attention and focus, the relationship can deepen and our responses to each other become rather permanent-feeling. If we move to a different job, a different neighborhood, the ties

CHAPTER 3

It's Time to Change Your Mind!

I said in the last chapter that repetition is one tool for changing even deep-seated beliefs, once we've done the work of discovering what they are to begin with; but obviously, before we get to techniques for change, we've got to figure out what's actually going on in the ole' thought factory. Discovery and awareness of one's own thought processes can be tricky, especially at the start. Like anything new, it can get easier with practice; but for the beginner, patterns that are hiding (from you) may be in plain sight (to others) and one of your most powerful allies can be a friend who won't sugar-coat their observations. Another is your willingness to weigh your every reaction against how it *feels*, rather than intellectualizing and trying to trace habits of thought back to their beginnings.

Let's talk about that first ally – the true friend, especially one who tends to be observant and trustworthy. I don't think I'll ever forget the time I was reading one of my Psych texts while attending San Jose State some years ago, when I turned to a man I had known for a few years and asked, "What do you think my hot button is? It says here, everybody has triggers that bypass the intellectual," and without pausing to weigh his answer, he said, "injustice. I think you have a real problem with any kind of injustice." This was not something we had ever discussed, nor had I noticed any such thing in myself; but after that, when I started to get outside myself, stand back, and start watching my own reactions to things I heard in the workplace or saw on T.V. I realized that, by God, he was right! And the feeling that went with it was a steely, quiet kind of anger.

I am still to this day not sure where that particular program came from or when some experience might have reinforced it, but I do know I can feel that sensation inside when I witness injustice. As it happens, I have made a conscious decision that rather than try to overwrite this particular thought/emotion reaction, I'll instead think in terms of choosing my battles. Not all injustices are equal, and until something warrants action on my part, I'll let that belief lie in the weeds like a trusted friend, because it may come to serve me in some specific instance. But what if it weren't something I believed could ever be helpful? What if, for instance, the hot button my friend pointed out had been that I tended to treat criticism with ice cream therapy?

If I were able to do that distancing thing, I might begin to connect that when my boss didn't think the report I turned in was detailed enough, or my current beau commented on heels making my legs look skinny, I felt inadequate, and wanted to grab a pint of French Vanilla and the biggest spoon I could find and disappear into primetime T.V. We've all heard of this kind of thing – some call it emotional eating; others call it self-medicating; but whatever the term, rather than treating the symptom (the latest diet, exercise of iron will, etc), we might do better by deciding to change the thoughts that lead to the emotion and its accompanying reaction.

Spoiler alert – here comes more good news. You can actually back into this, beginning with the reaction or the emotion, and affect change so that even if you can't figure out where the thought pattern started, you can loosen its grip. There are numerous ways to accomplish this, including the "processes" in the Hicks' book. Another of my favorites is what's called Emotional Freedom Technique, or EFT (aka Tapping), which is basically a self-administered form of acupressure, where you tap lightly on a series of energy meridians.

The way it works is, you verbally admit that something is making you angry, hurt, sad, fearful – whatever the painful emotion is – and you rate it on a scale of 1 where it's not that big a deal, to 10 where you feel totally helpless to change it. You say out loud that in spite of that feeling, you completely love and accept yourself. That's called the setup phrase, which you repeat as you tap with the fingers of one hand on the "karate chop" point of the other hand two or three times. Then, as you repeat a reminder phrase referring to the emotion, you tap on a set pattern of places on your face and body in a certain order: inner point of eyebrow, outer corner of eye, orbital bone under the eye, upper lip just under the nose, crease between lower lip and chin, just under the inner corner of the collar bone, under the arm a couple of inches below the armpit, and finally, on the top center of the head.

Yeah, I know this sounds a little weird; and trust me, if you were to walk into one of my classes and see a room full of people doing this you'd be *convinced*, but given how well it works, I'll take weird any day. I'll warn you that one part of it is tougher than it sounds and that's the setup phrase. "Even though I feel XYZ, I deeply and completely love and accept myself" may feel like a total lie! I mean really, love and accept myself when I let one individual's words push my buttons and make me want to smack her? Love and accept myself when I can't go more than a few steps up a ladder without shaking like a leaf? Here I am, pushing someone away who cares about me because he might lose interest and I want to leave the relationship first rather than get hurt, and *I'm supposed to love and accept myself?!* Uh huh, right – on what planet?!

Whether it feels like a lie at first or not, it's important to do this work, because whether we know where those feelings came from or not, they're there, banging around inside our heads (and yes, running us) and this is a way to work on letting them go so we can get on with creating the kind of life we want. I've seen demonstrations of this where people with long-standing fear, melancholy, guilt and in some cases mysterious physical ailments have suspended disbelief, and to say that the release of those emotions and the healing was dramatic is an understatement. I'd like to pause here and recommend you get hold of a film called The Tapping Solution by Nick Ortner. Nick's website is a treasure trove and there are tutorials and interviews with all sorts of experts that I hope will leave you with no doubt as to the effectiveness of the technique.

Later on, when we get into the connection between emotions and the quantum field, I think you'll see how important it is to address feelings, because they are far more powerful than any of us were raised believing. In a culture where the subject of emotions elicits either images of drama (seen any reality TV lately?) or out and out disdain (we're professional here – emotions have no place in this) we tend to want to shelve, stuff down, deny and look away from the very energetic parts of ourselves that make the difference between living "lives of quiet desperation" and having everything we want. I do not say that last part lightly. The essence of what can make our lives full, rich and yes – long and beautiful – is attainable if we are willing to assume responsibility for the power we have, and step up to the plate and use it well.

So, okay – let's talk about using thoughts and feelings well. One actual benefit, if you can call it that, of observing that certain things give you pain or anguish is that you can call that the negative space. People who do visual arts often point to the negative space as being just as important as the filled space, and that's absolutely true here, especially if you start your journey with lots of negative spaces. Most folks, if they're not really trying to stand back and watch their own feelings for any reason, tend to let inertia hold them in the down/hurt/angry space and basically it gets reinforced in exact proportion to how long they stay there and how often.

Ask the average person on the street what they want, and it can be hard to get a straight answer. They'll tell you a dozen things that they'd eliminate or change in their lives if they could and what they don't want. They're so focused on the down side that they're constantly revisiting and reliving (and reinforcing in the subconscious) all the things they don't like and don't want, and allowing no chance for changing those things themselves.

But here's a key - if something you don't like catches your notice, and rather than just sink into the automatic reaction, you pause for a beat and observe what caused the negative feelings, you can establish what it is that you *do want instead.* That sounds extremely simplistic and in a way it is, but it is also an extraordinarily large thing; because with this awareness, you now have the beginning of a new target upon which to start focusing your intent, your desire, your energies and with practice, a new neural pathway. So why don't more people take these steps and change their minds and lives? There too, old programming dies hard. We don't because we don't know we can, or how important it is.

My friend Eden has struggled with her weight since she left the military some twenty plus years ago. She's an excellent cook and is married to a man who not only appreciates her culinary skills but adores her regardless of her weight. The thing is, she's not happy with what she sees in the mirror, and issues of weight have actually had serious health implications for both of them. So what's holding her back?

For starters, she looks at the need to lose some 70-80 lbs, and the prospect of what it would take to affect such a huge change scares her. She fears that the self-discipline that would be required would be monumental and she chooses the familiar – however uncomfortable – rather than try and fail (again). I should say here that Eden's not an undisciplined or lazy person by any means. So what could she do differently?

Eden's idea of changing her habits enough to go back to her military weight strikes her as meaning she'd surely have to give up many of the comforts she enjoys, constantly depriving herself, and she adds to that the resistance she knows she'll get from her husband whose aversion to change runs even deeper. She doesn't like her current situation but she knows its parameters. They're not great but they don't scare her because they're familiar. No surprises lurk should she stay with the *status quo*.

She's staring up at a huge wall in front of her that represents the unfamiliar, and past performance has proven she's not a pole vaulter. But what would happen if she took the approach my former boss Dan did? I saw his picture and read his story in a wellness newsletter recently, and had it not been for recognizing the name, I never would have identified him.

This was a guy who used to inhale foot-long sandwiches every day at lunch, got no exercise at all, had a stressful position involving public safety that required split-second decision-making, and was easily more than a hundred pounds over what he should have weighed, even for his formidable height. He had a puffy red face, perpetually bloodshot eyes and a short fuse. In short, he was a poster child for imminent heart attack and/or stroke. But at some point, he decided to take some control in small, manageable increments – beginning with going for a walk.

The newsletter story about how he made gradual, steady changes read like a fairy tale, with Dan coming to his own rescue. The picture smiling out at me from the newsletter and the well-built guy who looked relaxed and happy were Dan's new version of himself – and that's the key about making big changes. Yes, it's possible for a person who tends to live life in the Miserable lane to have an epiphany that changes their heart and mind in an instant. It can and does happen, and people for whom it has, have watched their lives unfold like a flower they didn't know existed.

But far more common are the stories of people just like you and me who pick one small change they can make, work on it until it's automatic, and then pick another and then another. It works with habits of behavior, and it works with *habits of thought*. Let me give you an example from my own past that illustrates this (although at the time, I had no idea I was doing it right).

In 1989, I completed construction on a home I had designed and for which I had been General Contractor. If you've ever seen movies like (one of my favorites) The Money Pit, you've seen the sometimes humorous side of any kind of construction or renovation. It can be breathtaking at times and brutally life-consuming at others. The "dream home" I built took just about one year and was considered by many of the subcontractors who worked on it their highest achievement; but it had magnified the worst in my then-marriage and the weight of the responsibility coupled with feeling unappreciated for a lot of hard work had taken a toll on my health.

Shortly after completion, I developed a lung condition that put me on a teaching hospital's "dilemma of the month" list for three months running. Nobody could tell me what I had, but I was dying. I was told to get my affairs in order, as at the rate I was declining, I would be dead within three to four months. Me – who had been a distance athlete all my life – couldn't climb a flight of stairs. Rolling over in bed had become an aerobic exercise. It was incomprehensible.

I sat on my front veranda one soft, overcast day, thinking "here I am, living in my dream home – I have land around me with delicious pine trees and privacy, the wildlife come in close enough to see, l have horses in the pasture with their tails blowing gently in the breeze as I had always imagined... and I'm not going to live to see my 40th birthday." At that moment the phone inside the house rang and it was the doctor who had been treating me. He said they had identified the disease, and that while they could arrest its progress, they could not cure it.

In that moment, I made my mind up to be just as defiant as that bratty 8 year old who was not to be told she'd age the way her great aunt did. The rain that afternoon smelled especially delicious as I went back out to see the trees and the land with new eyes. I would find out what had caused this monstrous invader that had nearly cost me my dream, and I would win, but it would take a while.

As the electrostatic air cleaners were installed to run 24/7 and I received orders to remain indoors and never venture near the horses or the barn, I silently laid out a plan. I would *gradually* wean myself from the medications that made me feel as though I were a creature from another planet, begin spending a few minutes at a time with my beautiful animals, increasing the time verrrry gradually and little by little, defy the damned odds. I also delved into every kind of healing modality there were books about, determined that even if it were the smallest imaginable change for the good, I would make it.

Two years later, I took more than 100 hours of training to be a wildlife rehabilitator, got certified by both the State and Federal governments, and began taking in orphaned and injured wildlife of all kinds. I converted half of my stable into a little clinic, and spent long hours treating, caring for and videotaping the animals. At a follow-up doctor's appointment to satisfy my medical insurers, I was found to be disease free. The scar tissue that was supposed to be permanent no longer showed up on X-rays of my lungs nor on MRIs. Patience with a slow process and determination to let nothing stop me went a long way, over a long period of time.

During the slow weeks into months that I was healing, I was reading things like *The Nature of Personal Reality* and other Seth books by Jane Roberts, and getting a clue that there was a distinct connection between what we think, how it makes us feel, and how we can impact the kind of life we live through conscious decision. Some years later, books like *Excuse Me, Your Life Is Waiting* by Lynn Grabhorn and *Ask And It Is Given* by Esther and Jerry Hicks deepened and reinforced my understanding of the power of thought, feeling and manifestation.

It was not until after the year 2006 when, alone and starting from scratch on my own, did I start reading books about the connection between quantum physics and the relationship between human thought/feeling and the Infinite Field – or The Grid as it's sometimes called. That's when I realized what it was I had done in North Carolina, and how I could use it to change my life – albeit in increments that would have to be practiced until they supplanted old beliefs.

We often hear that the average person is using only 5-10% of their mental capacity; but what is meant is, we only recognize and "make use" of the conscious mind. The larger giant mind is the subconscious, and while yes, it was largely programmed with a belief soup during those vulnerable, unquestioning first five to six years, we can decide with the smaller conscious mind, to access the giant, examine what its programs are and gently, easily, lovingly persist in thinking and feeling new ways that get us where we want to be – in this case, splashing happily around in the Fountain of Youth.

Note that I say, *"persist* in thinking" and I believe this is key: we have to recognize that we get to choose the direction of our thoughts, and we must not believe they're hostage to whatever's going on around us. The old, initial reactions will persist for a while, but we must outlast them. The part about making changes, "gently, easily, lovingly" has become part of my own personal mantra, as has patience for the gestation all change requires.

Yes, as much as we might wish to make those quantum leaps from victim mentality to master, from miserable to merry, fat to thin, or *believing aging is a frightening, debilitating thing to knowing it can be fun, beautiful and juicy*, the path that more often sticks is learning new ways of approaching our issues (once we've figured out some of the major nasty programs) and turning them around, little by little. While taking more patience, this is *way* more comfortable for the auto-pilot-preferring subconscious. We can teach it new things to do automatically, little by little, just like we learned to hold a pencil, drink from a big kid's cup and brush our teeth.

Along the way, there are physical things we can do too, that will either support or sabotage what we want, and they work with thought/emotion processes like pieces of an interlocking puzzle. When we talk later about interconnectedness, we'll see that the food we take in, the water, the air we breathe – all are from the same source as our physical selves, and if we are to choose what is *optimal*, we must be vigilant there too, just as we are with becoming aware of thought and feeling patterns and choosing what our inner, instinctual selves will tell us is healthiest.

CHAPTER 4

The Power of Affirmations

I don't know of any single technique that has so many supporters – or has drawn so much fire – as the use of affirmations. The one I remember hearing when I was growing up was the one my grandparents recited that was a quote from early 20th Century psychotherapist Emile Coue.

"Every day, in every way, I am getting better and better." Think about that – we want to call affirmations something new or even "New Age" but once again, people who've been observant down through the ages have seen the power of affirmation and tried to harness its power. The trick is, that much like that setup statement I talked about when I described Tapping, we can try to make such grandiose statements about an improved state, that no matter how many times we repeat them, the now-present conscious mind (the one that wasn't formed yet when we were little and still checks out when we drift off to sleep) is hearing this stuff and going, "uh uh...nope...ain't so."

If I write down and repeat a hundred times a day, "I am five feet ten inches tall, brunette, and a runway model" the part of my consciousness that sees 5'5" in the full-length mirror with brown hair streaked blonde is probably not only going to yell, "liar!" but pay a lot less attention to anything else I try to affirm, so the good stuff doesn't get past the gate into the subconscious. But what if I try to find some statements that *are* true or that could be, upon which I can build? Suppose for instance, staying with the above runway model image, I note that models look confident and have the most amazing presence.

I might try saying, "I walk beautifully upright and take long, graceful steps," and "I wear clothes that make the most of my figure." Now, those are things that I may not think to do all the time, but if I start affirming them to myself – bringing my focus to them multiple times each day – there's a good chance my conscious mind is ok with them and will let them past the gate until eventually, doing exactly those things will become second nature. One of my favorite successes with this idea arose out of something I started about eight years ago, when I read a book about changing one's vision. A bit of history:

I started wearing glasses for near-sightedness in junior high – seventh grade, to be exact, when I was placed in the Accelerated 7A-1 Division. I had observed that the other smart kids in my classes nearly all wore glasses and as though by magic, I suddenly needed to sit in the front row or would find myself squinting to see the board. Gee, I wonder where my eyes got the idea they needed correction. Anyway, over the years, I dutifully accepted the increasingly stronger and stronger prescriptions that nearly everyone who wears glasses deals with. It never made sense to me that each new prescription felt odd and "pulled" on my eyes. This was supposed to help?! But my eyes adjusted and grew more dependent.

Fast forward to my early fifties when I read a book entitled, *The Program for Better Vision* by Martin Sussman. It reminded me of the (19th Century) Bates method, which I had seen work a minor miracle on a woman I knew in California. I loved the premise that no, it isn't necessary to get stronger prescriptions and be doomed to worsening eyesight over time. I also purchased and watched Meier Schneider's *Yoga for Your Eyes*, and set about finding an optometrist who'd work with me. When I told the pretty young woman I was seeing for the first time what I wanted to do, she said "I don't think it'll work, but it's your money...."

Over the ensuing four years, I followed the techniques in the book and video, returning to my skeptical but willing optometrist once or twice a year to get my prescription kicked back a quarter diopter in one eye or the other; and each time I put my latest pair of glasses on, I'd say to myself, "these glasses are weaker than the last pair! How cool!"

It was a true statement, my conscious mind registered that what was happening was real and measurable, and I celebrated and appreciated each new, weaker prescription. And yes, each pair felt a little funny for the first few days just as stronger and stronger prescriptions had in the past; but I was moving in the right direction, and saying my little affirmation every day focused and congratulated my eyes on their improvement. I will tell you, by the way, that when I asked my optometrist to look back over my chart last year, even she was impressed. I had gone from a correction of 3.0 in one eye and 2.75 in the other to 1.0 in both eyes. No surgery. Nothing invasive. And most importantly, *no doubt in my mind that it would work.*

Stop here and think for a moment about how you might use this kind of affirmation where the whole business of aging is concerned. The first thing it might help you to know is that no less than Einstein himself proved that there is no such thing as objective time. He called it "an illusion, albeit a persistent one." What that means is that while we measure experience based upon the predictable revolutions of our gorgeous planet around a star, there is actually no such thing as time. We pass through and participate in *experience*, but time does not pass. Einstein and others have pointed out that what the *idea* of time does is give us a way to organize our lives. That's all. It's an agreement. Interesting, huh?

Something else to consider is what economist John Galbraith identified as "revised sequence marketing" which is where people who want to sell you something cook up some kind of issue they can talk you into believing is natural so they can sell you the solution. If they can make you believe that as a guy over 40 you're probably having (inevitable, unavoidable) issues in the bedroom, you need their pill. If you're a woman past 50, you're going to be slouched over and breaking hips if you don't take their pill.

If you're aware of what's going on though, you don't have to buy into it. Period.

If you don't have some affirmations you know you can believe about aging in particular, you might try some that are sort of "training wheels" to begin with:

"I'm working on clearing out old beliefs."

"I'm getting clear on what I want from experience."

"Einstein was a pretty bright guy – I like this idea about time being an illusion."

"I'm taking small steps and having fun with this."

Make your affirmations just that – affirmative and in the present – and give yourself some leeway. As you see improvements in specific markers, congratulate yourself and aim for the next thing as though it were a goal:

"It's so neat that my vision has improved! I bet I can ….<fill in the blank>

Make note of even the smallest successes – celebrate them. Congratulate yourself and *have fun with it*. Make a game of looking for and noticing your attitude, body and even the circumstances surrounding you changing for the better. This is a wild ride and every bit of it is yours to enjoy.

CHAPTER 5

The "F" Word Or What's Foooood Got to Do, Got to Do With It? (with loving apologies to Tina Turner)

OK, so at this point, you might be asking, "If the way my body looks and feels turns out to be the result of what's in my head, what does food have to do with any of it? Can't I just 'think and feel' my way to young and healthy?" Some Law of Attraction advocates would say yes, and there could be some validity to that when we consider the total miracles of healing, regeneration and more that have been worked by mind over matter. I sat in an Abraham-Hicks seminar one day a few years ago, and heard Abraham say that people could live on popsicles if they wanted to. Now, it was a hot, muggy day in Washington, DC and the hotel's air conditioning system was having issues, so the thought of downing a half-dozen popsicles held some serious appeal; but truthfully, having studied both physiology and human nutrition, I don't think that would be workable – at least *not for long*. And even if you could do that, why would you *want* to? Don't you want to show some love to the body temple you've been given to live and cruise around in?

I think that if you're going to approach rejuvenation the way that is most harmonious for bodies *and* minds (and yes, food affects your thinking and feelings) you do need to consider what you're fueling yourself with, and here's why: all those wonderful little cells that make up your organs (and those brain-generated peptides that give the cells their marching orders, as we discussed earlier) are created from molecules you take in, in the form of food, air and water. I'm sure you've heard and maybe yourself used the phrase, "garbage in, garbage out" and it doesn't take a rocket scientist to figure out that this doesn't only apply to computer software. What blows me away is that an extraordinary amount of what people think is just fine to feed themselves and their families is actually non-food; and that even the stuff the homemakers' magazines tout as "balanced" is often deceivingly good-looking pictures of dishes arranged by "food stylists," in ads paid for by big-business food producers.

I'm going to ask you once again to stop and notice. Really look closely and see the bill of goods we're all being sold by people who make their living selling inferior products that pass for food. OK – another list: get out another piece of paper and watch TV for one hour. Watch in particular the ads for restaurants and fast food. Notice the colors (mostly all goldens, reds and "pops" of green.) Looks like real food, doesn't it?! Appealing, wholesome…. Now go on the websites of those same places or products and look up the nutritional content of the foods you saw advertised. Please…I know I'm being a pain, but this is important – this is your and your families' bodies you're feeding with this stuff! When you regain consciousness and your heart starts beating normally again, ask yourself if you had any clue. Saturated fat? Salt? Preservatives? Dyes? Look at the ingredients you can't pronounce, and ask yourself if you believe you're going to stay young or get that way again ingesting this stuff on a regular basis.

I was reading an article in a major online news source recently that highlighted a spate of serious birth defects that nobody wanted to come right out and blame on nearby orchards being sprayed with herbicides and pesticides, nor on the well water near them that may have also been contaminated. We half-heartedly joke about the Standard American Diet (SAD indeed) as though we don't *really* have to be concerned, and a room full of otherwise educated, intelligent people who get to talking about their families' eating habits will almost invariably turn to little LuLu's favorite boxed mac 'n cheese or Aunt Cecily's sugar-laden treat that the entire family (for how many generations?) considers an "absolute necessity" at the holidays. And then there's the 6 yr old boy who won't eat anything but burgers and fries. His mother smiles indulgently, "he's such a picky eater." Note – he's dictating to his parents rather than the other way around, and they cave to keep him from fussing. Really?!? They give in to a kid who'll eventually get hungry enough to eat the wallpaper off the walls if they just hold out rather than make themselves unpopular for a few meals?

The fact is, the kid watches what the parents think is good or that he sees on TV, tries it - wanting to emulate the parent or TV ideal - and next thing you know, it's a well-worn neural path. It's a belief about what is preferred, and it is not doing the kid any favors. If it's not a good belief, then we've got ourselves *and* our kids to turn around, and the greatest teacher is example. The differences in the nutrient content of fast food vs standard home-cooked vs *optimal* is huge. The difference in the toxin levels of conventionally grown/raised food vs organic is also huge. When I say "optimal" I do mean whole, unprocessed and wherever possible organic. And yes, organic stuff costs more, and spending for quality food and cooking at home needs to become a bigger priority than data plans and X number of pair of shoes. (okay - sorry – I get wound a little tight on this subject, but this strikes me as injustice and you *know* how well I handle that!)

Your heart and soul are riding around in a magnificent vehicle – the outward manifestation of everything you think and feel and take in, *psychologically and physically*. Are you going to feed your Ferrari some cheap, back-alley gas? Not me. I want to fire on all twelve cylinders and hear my engine purr like a big, gorgeous cat because I fuel it well. And folks, none of us have to be wealthy to do that, contrary to public opinion. Truth be told, most people who say they can't afford to eat healthy *have never actually tried it*. It is a matter of priority, period. Just like stopping to think about your mental processes and emotional reactions, you have to be willing to support your transformation on every front including your nourishment. You can't be on auto-pilot/ trance setting when you choose what to eat.

Let me get a few things about food out on the table (pardon the pun) and make them clear. While Nutrition actually is an amazing science with lots of nuances that most folks never have to learn, there are some basics *everyone* should understand:

1. People can get all the protein they need from plants, and most people in industrialized nations get far too much. Any time you put a legume with a whole grain, you've got a complete protein and a few plant sources, like quinoa, soy and hemp have the whole package. Before you scrunch up your nose, I suggest you think in terms of "acquired tastes." Some of the most sophisticated people in the world who are experts on food and wine have *acquired* their tastes for their favorites, so as you think about your protein choices, consider that making changes could be your own kind of cultural growth.

I am not advocating that you live on flavorless tofu or anything else that's bland and uninteresting – vegetarianism has gone so mainstream that finding magazines, books, online articles and even entire TV channels devoted to eating well without eating meat is easy and a win-win all around, not to mention being a strike in favor of the environment. The resources in terms of land, water and (again, conventionally grown) grains that go into the large-scale raising of food animals are extraordinary, and their misuse is wasteful and contributes to pollution on a lot of levels.

Most people don't want to hear the horror stories about what happens in feed lots and slaughter houses, and films like *Food, Inc* can leave painful tracks on your mind; but at least consider what gets passed on to your body chemically when you consume conventionally raised animals. I lived for a few years in a region with heavy conventional poultry production, and it was not unusual to see kids no more than nine or ten years old already starting to get wide across the beam and developing breasts (boys as well as girls, folks). If that doesn't make you wonder about their food and water (and all those rapid-growth hormones) I don't know what will.

A close cousin of eating animals is the consumption of dairy products. I remember sitting in a human nutrition class years ago, and watching with interest as the instructor put a line graph up on the screen showing from highest to lowest the consumption of dairy products worldwide. The U.S. was up near the top, as were some of the northern European countries like Germany and the Scandinavian nations, while down at the lower end were Asian nations, including Japan. The instructor then overlaid that graph with a transparent second graph, showing from highest to lowest the incidences of breast cancer. Do I have to complete this paragraph? My stomach started to feel queasy, and to this day, I shake my head in frustration every time I see ads of otherwise saavy people wearing white moustaches.

I will simply suggest here that you do some research into the traditional foods of Japan and consider that it is only in the cities that have become Westernized and the food intake influenced by Western predilections for meat and dairy that heart attack, stroke and cancer have risen since the end of World War II, when the island nation made peace and began exchanging cultural values with us.

2. If you don't like veggies, that's probably more programming running you. Try new things, in small amounts, keeping in mind that while your taste buds may take some training to acquire new tastes, *your body adores them*. And it's not just any veggies – there's a good reason I'm a strong advocate of organic, and a non-profit organization called The Environmental Working Group publishes a list each year of the Clean Fifteen and Dirty Dozen that makes choosing the good stuff easier. The Clean Fifteen are fruits & veggies that, even if conventionally grown, don't have as many toxins, while the Dirty Dozen (which has grown to more than a dozen now) are those that tend to be loaded with chemicals even if they're washed and/or peeled. People in my classes that I've given copies of the list to are always shocked.

None of us wants to think that those beautiful shiny apples we say will keep the doctor away, or the big, sweet strawberries we delight in handing to a toddler could be anything but pure, healthy bliss; but trust me, if you saw guys in hazmat suits spraying the orchards and fields, and big trucks full of refuse from those (hormone-laden) poultry houses pulling up to "fertilize" the ground, you'd have to stop and give it a second look. Do you want to see if you'll be keeping a regular family doc away, or would you like to go straight to an oncologist?

Again, so much of what we believe about choices we're making is actually assumptions that have been made for us. As hard as it sounds to start thinking differently about what you put on the table and in your mouth, I promise you, it does get easier. Like anything else, practice leads to new – hopefully healthier - habits. I had the advantage of having been raised in a family of health nuts, but they had to learn after diseases showed up that no medical professional had reasons for. I had to learn, and you can too. For myself, my own "practice" is to carry the Clean Fifteen & Dirty Dozen list folded up in my purse so it's with me when I shop. I make sure I get at least 5 servings a day (oh, c'mon – a serving is only half a cup!) of veggies that are either organic or conventionally grown but on the Clean list, and one or two of fruit.

If there's something I like and it's out of season and only available from overseas (and grown who-knows-how) then I forego it and wait. Asparagus is all the more precious a treat because I can only get it local and organic in the Spring, and when the organic sweet potatoes come in during the Fall and Winter, I make everything from soup to smoothies with them. What I save by not buying meat and packaged things, I can spend on organic produce and have enough money left to treat myself to a little bouquet of flowers or a precious pint of raw cashews. True, I do *not* have the latest in every electronic gadget or receive every cable TV channel known to man – I prefer to literally put my money where my mouth is – on good nourishment. And while we're on the subject of optimal food...

3. Get away and *stay* away from refined sugars, ALL artificial sweeteners, and trans-fats. Anywhere, any time. I hope I haven't made myself unclear. If you don't know where they hide or what their aliases are, again, there are some good resources in the back of this book and I'll cover them on my website, <u>healthnutliving.com</u>. I saw a statistic recently about how cavemen consumed probably the equivalent of 33 teaspoonsful of sugar in some form or other over the course of a year, while the average kid now consumes more than that *every day*. What part of kids and adults taking medications (more damned chemicals!) for ADD and ADHD are we not connecting with what they eat?! Okay, okay – I know I've gotta' let the injustice thing take a break – bear with me.

Something else you should know though is that plentiful sugar in the bloodstream tends to bond with protein molecules, causing them to connect, or "cross-link" with other protein molecules. This cross-linking makes the tissues these protein molecules are part of stiffen. The more sugar, the more cross-linking, and the harder the tissues become. What are the most obvious outer signs of the way we think of an aged body? Do we think of flexibility and fluidity? And there's more.

One last scary thing about sugar is that, like excess protein, plentiful sugar tends to make the body acidic. Studies into the environments in the body that tend to enable the rapid growth of cancer cells seem to point to acidity as a major culprit. Somewhat more alkaline body environments are healthier all around, and a largely plant-based diet (i.e. veggies, legumes and a modest amount of fruit) produce that effect. If you'd like to see where you fall on the scale, get yourself some urine Ph test strips and tinkle on a strip a couple of times a day. Experiment with upping your veggie intake and cutting out sugar and watch the colors go in the right direction. See? Some science is easy!

4. If you honestly don't know how to cook, go online or get a good, basic book (see reading list) and *learn!* Nobody's asking you to become the Iron Chef – just learn how to make some basic stuff with some herbs and spices for interest – and you'll be surprised (again, little incremental changes) at how good minimally manipulated food tastes. Raw foods are another gift from the health gods, and I wish I had known how good fresh veggie juices and sprouted foods tasted years ago. They're also a godsend for the cooking-averse who still want to be healthy. For a truly wild and inspiring story of the healing and rejuvenating power of raw foods and juices, watch the video, *Fat, Sick and Nearly Dead* by Joe Cross. He also has a website called Rebooting With Joe that's fabulous, as is Kris Carr's Crazy Sexy site.

5. Drink plenty of clean water. We hear it all the time and some people have made it a good habit while others, like a woman I coached a few years back, felt she was getting all the fluids she needed with four to six soft drinks a day. I will only say that her skin was pasty and she looked as though she were 7 months pregnant. All the time. If you must have flavor in your water to enjoy it (more crappy programming) try the juice of half a lemon and if you have an incurable sweet tooth at the beginning, start off with a couple of teaspoonsful of agave or maple syrup or, better yet, a pinch of stevia and cut back gradually to where you can actually appreciate the taste of pure, unadulterated water. Again – little, incremental changes.

6. Finally, be very wary of fad diets. I know – if you're 20-30 lbs or more overweight, it is extraordinarily tempting to want to go with whatever seems fast, especially if it's being touted on late night TV by people with M.D. after their names. I will go out on a limb here and tell you something I don't think is commonly known: medical doctors are not typically required to learn anything at all (either as pre-med or in med school) about nutrition. Veterinarians are, but not medical doctors. Weird, huh?

Little side story: in the mid-'90s, when I was in the pre-Vet program at North Carolina State, I discovered as so many hopeful would-be animal docs did, that it was incredibly more difficult to get into vet school than med school. The pre-vet program had all sorts of requirements that a lot of med schools didn't (including at least one course in some kind of Nutrition) and for those students who tried and failed to get admitted to the vet school, there was the ironic offer, "well, there's always med school...."

That said, some docs have made it their business to learn a lot about healthy lifestyle practices including good nutrition but the vast majority have not. Some of the recommended books listed in the Reading List are authored by the former. You know which I'd prefer you seek out.

While we're here in the chapter on food, I promised earlier I was going to cover some points on removing toxins from the body, and I'd like to relate a story that jumped out at me when I was studying anatomy and physiology. There have apparently been experiments done wherein living tissues have been kept alive for long periods of time, only finally degrading and dying when the byproducts of metabolism were not removed. In other words, when nobody took out the trash. If proper nourishment is provided and inflammation is kept to a minimum, the cells are happy to cruise along, doing amazing, complex jobs including reproducing, and even cells that have been damaged (again, often by inflammation) can be restored to perfect functionality by removing the irritating condition.

We hear the term "anti-inflammatory" all the time, but we have been trained to think in terms of chemical intervention. Pills for headaches, ointments for aches and pains – those are the anti-inflammatories that leap to mind (you're undoubtedly getting tired of me referring to programming, so I'll stop for the moment); but watch my mouth: sugar, too much protein, and the stress chemicals the brain produces in response to what we're thinking and feeling down the negative side of the emotional scale are all inflammatory. Take those out of the equation and remember to take out the trash so the cells aren't clogged with their own waste products, and you have a dynamic, joyfully functional bunch of cells, keeping you alive, young, and gorgeous.

OK, so I admit it -- I will absolutely own that this is a gross oversimplification of what's going on in the body; but the fact is, you have a few simple choices to make – there's that word again – and the commodity that's hanging in the balance between what things you choose is your body. You get to decide what you put your thoughts on and how you guide them to what feels good, and you also get to decide what you put in and on your body to either promote the dynamics of its constant regeneration or not. I'll leave you with this quotation from the text book that was required for my study of the human body:

"Cell aging is a complicated process with many causes, but to be perfectly frank, the precise reason an otherwise healthy person grows old and dies is still a mystery."[1]

---

[1]   *Human Anatomy & Physiology*, E.N. Marieb, RN, PhD and K. Hoehn, MD, PhD Pearson Education, Inc

CHAPTER 6

Nothing happens until something moves.

- Albert Einstein

Move! Move! Move! Move!

- My 9th grade gym teacher

I read an article some time back that I wish I could quote directly, where the author said he had found himself seated on a plane next to a mature, well-dressed man – someone obviously in good shape who looked strangely familiar. The man turned out to be Jack La Lanne, and when asked what he felt was the secret to his staying young, he said "exercise." Knowing what I know now, I might have enjoyed carrying on a spirited, fun debate had I been there, insisting that the secret is the way a person thinks, believes and intends; but the facts around getting regular exercise are not matters of theory, and the two ideas are not at all mutually exclusive. I have decades of personal experience with the power of exercise to not only affect positive change in my body, but in the way I think and how I *feel* on an emotional level. There's that word again. Feel. And it's incredibly important.

I don't think I was ever so amazed at the human body's capabilities, even with the afore-related tale of my own self-healing firmly affixed in my psyche, as I was when I started studying anatomy and physiology. The wisdom in each cell – not just organs or organ systems, but the tiny, individual little cells that form communities and change according to what the body needs to maintain "stasis" or balance – had me texting the man in my life late at night "shouting" in all caps how freaking *amazing* it all was. Did you know, for instance, that there's a particular type of bone cell that will lay down bone matrix, hang around for a while waiting to see if it can leave the bone tissue as is or have to adjust its mineral content, and then turn itself into a different kind of bone cell?

I don't know – maybe that doesn't do much for you; but the more I learned, the more awed I became at this miracle we form, live in and eventually release called our bodies. We take in those "molecules" that the body needs in the food, air and water we need, and the body's wisdom knows what to do with them! New cells are formed, the ones that have carried out their purpose die off and are sloughed off, and the new cells carry on all their functions, including repair and growth. And here's where the idea of "wear and tear" runs contrary to the way cells work if they're provided with what they need (including an absence of inflammation).

You've probably heard that some cells, like those of the lining of your mouth, turn over every day. Muscle cells take a few days, and you can see the result of their repair and growth when "muscle definition" develops as a result of exercise. Bones take the longest. Sooner or later though, after something like seven years, the body you see in the mirror is an entirely different one that has been constantly formed and re-formed by this amazing process of regeneration. Wrap your mind around that one – you can have a whole different version of your body in the course of a few months into years, unless you sabotage the process.

The biggest and most important message here in this chapter and in the previous one on nutrition is that bodies are not static. They are communities of cells forming organs and organ systems, and the whole of it all, coalescing into what we call the body, is meant to change and move. We are not a collection of the same kind of cells that make up a rock, which is in a fixed place and has no need for joints (though under an electron microscope, we'd see that the rock too is a mass of energy, just vibrating differently from our bodies).

One of the scenes I liked best in the film, *The Secret*, was the description of the body being made up of a mass of energy, "operating in a larger energy field." If you look at the way the body is designed, it is made for movement, not only in terms of the inner workings of organ systems, such as the blood being pumped around by our hearts, or food pushed through the alimentary canal by the undulating movement of muscle tissues called peristalsis; but also, things that rely on movement of the whole body to work optimally, such as the limbic fluids secreted by glands that have no "veins" to transport them. They rely on our moving our bodies to provide the pumping action. And what gives us the ability to move? Joints! Muscles! Our bodies are made for movement, inside and out, and one of the most important gifts exercise can give us is that positive effect on our feelings which again ties back to what parts of the DNA the cells activate.

Now, I don't think there are a lot of folks who haven't heard the phrase, "beta-endorphin high" but I'd like to ask, by a show of hands, how many of us have experienced it? How many do on a regular basis? I will confess here, that while writing this book, I have at some points used the dearth of time I have available as an all-too-convenient excuse not to get out and at least walk if not work out. And I have paid the price. I don't get that feeling of inner *and outer* glow – the reward for getting a bit out of breath and sweating a little (or a lot) that is my body's gift exchange with my mind and emotions when I've done what they both want.

Mind you, when I was trying to get back into shape after a too-long hiatus with my exercise program, there were mornings when I hated Jillian Michaels, bouncing up and down and admonishing me, "don't you dare phone this in!" from my TV screen; but as with so many of the other things we've talked about here, it got easier the more I did it. I had started off with baseline measurements and had promised myself to stay off the scale any other day but Sunday. I wrote down everything I put in my mouth (again, awareness is power) and when I had good results, I celebrated them with entries in a little journal I carry around with me where I keep track of cool stuff that happens (more about that later).

On the days when I couldn't get up early to work out because it would mean trying to make it through a full day on less than 6 hours of sleep, I didn't feel as good. I loved that I was getting into my prettier, more stylish clothes again, but I missed the chemical happiness rush that so often carried me through at least the first half of every day if not longer. I've recommended the movie, *What the Bleep* earlier in this book, and if you watch it, you'll pick up on the fact that we can become addicted to certain feelings that are actually chemicals generated by our own bodies. Beta-endorphins are among those chemicals, and they truly can become addictive. The good and even better news is, there is absolutely nothing wrong with getting your body conditioned to crave the chemicals that feel so good from exercise.

Yes, it means you'll be a bit edgy or disappointed when you can't exercise; but it also means you're reaching for increasing levels of fitness, and let's face it folks, what's hotter than a body (of any age!) that's in great shape?! One of the prettiest, most in-shape women I ever met was a contract trainer. We shared a cubicle, and since we did the same kind of work, we often observed each other in a classroom situation. We ate much the same way (what's commonly known as "eating clean") but there was a big difference in the way each of us looked. I was slender and toned – she was even more slender with muscle definition and perfect proportions. The difference? She worked out every day, often twice a day, in order to compete at a professional level in Figure and Fitness. The difference was the level and intensity of exercise, but we were both pictures of calm and we each had a positive attitude.

Now, I know I'm going to sound like a broken record here, saying "small, incremental changes" but I'd invite you to think back to my story about my old boss, Dan. He didn't go out and start training for marathons at the beginning – he just decided to go for a walk! And it can be just that small a change for you too, especially if your favorite way to unwind right now is to plant yourself in front of the tube or computer and veg out. Just make the decision to try, for say a few days – three or four, maybe – to spend ten minutes doing something involving movement instead of sitting. Walk. Dance. Jump rope. Anything that will get your heart rate up a little and have you breathing just a little more vigorously.

I'm not saying you have to abandon your BFF recliner and turn into Tony Horton, but just try for ten minutes a day, before you go and sit down, to do something – anything – involving moving around. If you like the way it makes you feel (or can at least get used to it) after a few days to a week, try for fifteen to twenty minutes for the next week after that. The thing that makes any kind of exercise stick – something you'll continue to do until it becomes part of that auto-program you live in – is that it's something you either totally like or are *interested in learning* to do. If you've never taken yoga, try that, perhaps, or Tai Chi. Or if you've never tried workout routines, browse the hundreds of exercise DVDs that are out there. Everything from lighthearted dance-type routines to hard-core cardio/strength circuit training can start you at any level of fitness you're at and move you forward. Pick something that looks like fun! The more you like it, the easier it is to make it a habit. Once it becomes a habit – well, to say you've hit an upward spiral is an understatement.

Remember my story about my lungs and how I got past giving any more airtime to sickness than I had to? Well, that journey started the Spring before I turned 40. Seven years later I moved to a different state and my way of coping with the stress of starting my life over on a number of fronts was to go out and walk/jog, very slowly at first, around one city block. One block became two, and the next thing I knew, I was pushing myself to do a whole mile…then a mile and a half…. At age 51, I entered my first 5K (not knowing it was cross-country, after I had been training on nice flat streetscapes) and took 3rd place in my age group. I still have that trophy in my study and I look at it every day. Running uphill toward the finish line that day had started four years earlier with getting up one morning and going outside. I had a pair of running shoes on my feet and a determination not to let circumstances ruin everything I knew I had to look forward to.

There's something I need to say here. I know there may be people reading this book who are wheelchair-bound or in some other way infirmed and it may be that the most movement you can get in is perhaps rhythmically waving your arms to music. It's still movement and I encourage you to do it, no matter how small you think it is. I'd also like to point you to another rather miraculous story of a man whose body was broken in so many places, his doctors were convinced he'd be unable to move or even breathe on his own after a horrendous accident. If you can, either read or watch the story of Morris Goodman, who is known as The Miracle Man.

Morris, who was also featured in the movie *The Secret*, crashed a plane in March of one year. He was in a coma for a while, and when he woke, found that he couldn't breathe without a respirator, his neck and back were broken, and at one point, could only blink his eyes in response to a nurse pointing to letters on an alphabet card. Morris had been a fan of the motivational/inspirational Zig Ziegler, and believed that what he decided for himself – how he directed his thoughts – could win over any diagnosis the medical community might deliver. He decided that by Christmas of that same year, he would walk out of the hospital on his own. And he did.

As you can imagine, Morris did a lot of mind work – listening to his body and communicating with it deliberately – consciously – not letting the naysayers have the last word or define him. A quote of Morris' from the film was, "once you have your mind, you can put things back together again," but it is also a fact that he probably wouldn't have gotten anywhere near the front door of the hospital and gotten up out of the wheelchair without a lot of physical therapy (movement!) and the persistent belief in himself that was no doubt being aided and abetted by brain chemicals. Morris said he saw himself walking out of that hospital and he did whatever it took to regenerate his body.

He visualized his healing, and like Olympic athletes who have come back from injuries of all kinds by mentally rehearsing and stepping into the success of their events, healed his body. His story is nothing short of what we think of as miraculous, but I would submit to you that the only reason more people don't do what Morris Goodman did is because *they don't know they can.* The body and mind must work in concert to produce significant change. They must. So let's talk some more about visualization, shall we? It is one of the most powerful tools in your arsenal if you are to reset your biological clock to its sweet spot and stay there.

CHAPTER 7

Whhhhoooooo are you?

- a hookah-smoking caterpillar

Where were you on September 11? I've never met anyone
who says they can't remember, or who doesn't hear the date
mentioned and can tell you exactly where they were and how
they first heard about the destruction of the World Trade
Center. It gripped the hearts of people around the world,
and there are some that still today have not been able to get
past the trauma, either because they had some connection
with people who were hurt or killed, or because they still
replay the terrible scenes on TV in their minds, to where it
has become a deeply worn memory path. Staying in such a
mind habit, reliving the destruction is in itself destructive
to mind and body.

It is my hope that this extreme example will serve to remind
you briefly of the extraordinary heroism of the people who
responded so valiantly that day and in the weeks and months
afterward; but more, to take you forward from that sad place

to understanding the power of visualization and how you can put it to its most creative and beautiful use.

Here's another exercise for you: If you have a photo album or a box of pictures, poke through them and see if there's at least one picture that draws forth some kind of positive emotion, especially if it's an action shot involving you or some people you were with. Were you on vacation someplace? Were you standing close to someone you loved? Did someone just fall off their water skis and came up laughing? Good – now, close your eyes and do your best to go back to that time. It doesn't matter whether it was last week or decades ago – just step into that time and place. Allow yourself to fully remember, *from inside the picture*, reliving as many details of it it *with as many of your senses* as you can.

I have a picture of my son at about age 4, smiling at me from the passenger-side seat of my car. He's wearing a navy blue quilted jacket with a hood that has fake fur around the edge, and when I get myself back into the driver's side, it's a cold afternoon in Akron, Ohio. I have my old Instamatic in my hand, intending to use up the last shots on a roll of film, and I've just picked up my boy from the sitter's house. My nose and fingers are cold, I can hear the engine of my AMC Gremlin idling, and I'm looking forward to going home to our second-floor apartment and setting up the aluminum Christmas tree the landlord and his wife gave us. If I stay in the picture long enough, the scene morphs to where I string the single set of tiny twinkle lights I could afford on the tree and plug it in. A 4th of July sparkler springs to life, and Shawn and I laugh and hug at how amazing it is....

That was just over forty years ago, and I can still enjoy that event by envisioning it. What's more, when I do, my brain chemicals are bathing my body's cells with happy juice (and you know how good that is) because the *subconscious mind doesn't know that I'm remembering*. It takes whatever I focus on as fact and responds exactly the same way as it would if I were living the event now. Please re-read that sentence and repeat after me: "the subconscious doesn't know if it's real or pretend." Any time you can visualize, whether from the trigger of a photo, hearing a song, or (probably the most powerful and unexpected) a certain smell, you are living that scenario at some level and your subconscious *responds in kind*. Do it a lot and it becomes a thought habit. Do you see where I'm going with this?

Visualization, whether replaying positive memories or scripting imaginative new scenarios, is a way of deeply reinforcing healthy, happy neural pathways and overwriting the saboteurs that are carrying on the old, destructive monologues that our bodies are bound to obey. Morris Goodman's story is a perfect example of visualization used for healing. Morris says in the movie, *The Secret*, that he saw himself "walking out of that hospital, being a normal person again". Mind you, he had pretty much every doctor who came in contact with him telling him that what he intended was not possible; but Morris didn't own their diagnoses any more than I owned having to live in a jail defined by the walls of my home and its air cleaners twenty-five years ago.

So, how does a person start visualizing? Some people do it easily, and it's just a matter of training the pictures to be positive rather than lolling back to the latest argument with the brother-in-law or the near-miss on the drive home. For both those folks and the visualization-challenged, there are some easy and very cool, fun things to try, the first being the use of pictures and words in print – not necessarily of good things from the past, but even things that we'd like to create for perhaps the first time! Have you come across images in decorating or design magazines of houses or gardens that take your breath away? Do you see ads for the local gym and admire the toned bodies? Do the newsletters you get pertaining to your profession show confident, well-dressed people sitting comfortably in their offices or perhaps outside, blueprints in hand watching a building being constructed?

It doesn't have to be something that's already been part of your life in the past – you're identifying here what you want. If you want to be youthful, having fun, engaged in doing fun things and enjoying a life filled with energy and joy, find those pictures. This is not a new idea, nor would I ever claim it as an original – the notions of "treasure mapping" and "vision boards" have been around for more than a century. They are tools that provide visual clues we can step inside, whether they are reminders of a happy past or entirely new, desired results we wish to create.

My own vision boards are made of cork, and I tend to place differently focused ones where I'll be doing something pertinent; for example, I have one on the wall near my computer where I write, with a clipped out copy of the New York Times masthead and the word Bestsellers from the book section. To me, this is a connection to the idea of reaching lots of people with a message I know can help them. In my family room where the TV is and where Jillian and Tony put me through my paces, I have a small board with a few pictures of healthy, toned women I've cut out of magazines, and I spend a little time as often as possible, seeing myself reaching that optimal level of fitness.

Does this give you an idea of how to apply this to your own body where aging (or not) is concerned? Obviously, we're not talking about going back to being a high-schooler (really, would you want to?!) but if you have a picture of yourself at an age when you felt marvelously comfortable in your own skin, or if not, a picture of someone you *perceive* as feeling that way, use it as a trigger. Write a whole script around it, just as though you were producing a mini-movie, about how it feels to be in that life. Cut out words from magazines and newspapers that are happy, exciting and affirming and put those with the pictures.

Climb inside it – don't just look at it from the outside as though you're watching yourself – you do enough of that to register how you react to things – this is you being in your own ideal picture and you must live it for a while as often as possible or you won't be engraving the experience of it in those neural pathways. Remember, what you're after is being able to make the experience so detailed and real that your blessed subconscious is swept along with the beauty of it, and those cells that make up your body are being bathed in joyous youth juice. Like attracts like.

There is one element to doing this work that I believe is appropriate to mention here, and if you'll bear with me, it will take us into the space where the mind and the Quantum Field interact: there is no such thing as "no" to either the subconscious mind or the Field. In other words, when we visualize or write affirmations or repeat a mantra, the words "won't, don't, no, and not" don't work as we think they would. Yes, what I remember about my early my programming (girls aren't good at math) would seem like a contradiction, but if what I received was actually "girls struggle with math" or "girls are bad at math" then what the people who do brain entrainment and subliminal recordings tell us confirms this. Their message is that whatever the focus is on, carries -- negations don't register.

So how does this affect the way we create our scripts and affirmations? We have to leave the "don't" and "won't" out of the language and the picture. In other words, focus on what you don't want only long enough to figure out what its opposite is and run with that. If my friend Eden wants to lose weight, she leaves the negation of needing to lose something out of her picture. She builds a script around being in a state of becoming her perfect size and how delicious it feels to slip into those size 6 clothes again. She envisions choosing elegant little portions of healthy, beautifully prepared food, seeing her gorgeous reflection in the mirror at the health club where she works out, and giving away all the clothes that are far too big for her. Do you see the difference?

Regardless of what you want to change in your life, sages from as far back as history has been recorded have told us to imagine, and to as great an extent as possible, *spend time in* the desired vision in every detail, and it cannot help but come to fruition. This becomes a key idea to changing the way the body/mind has come to expect the chain of events known as aging to go. Part of this obviously is getting the subconscious (again, through repetition to where it's on auto-pilot) convinced that this vision is in process, so that it goes to work producing those all-important brain chemicals your cells respond to.

The other part – the part that has fascinated scientists since they stepped outside Newtonian physics and began exploring the quantum world – is the energetic effect each and every one of us is having on the dynamic, always-moving quantum field. The spiritual leaders of 3,000 B.C. wrote in terms appropriate to their time and place "…as above, so below… as within, so without." What's on the inside becomes what's on the outside.

CHAPTER 8

Keeping the Programming All Good

Let's say you're determined not to let your body fall into the trap of false advertising (which whether they mean to or not, most of the people around you are buying into and passing on as gospel). You examine where you got your ideas about aging, like early programming, and decide to forgive all the people, movies, overheard whispers, half-understood body language, etc. and realize it was just folks passing on what they had been taught. I say forgive, because it can be easy to fall into the trap of getting angry and resentful for any negative stuff your early caretakers passed on, and hanging onto those feelings is toxic. You don't have to condone anything that was said or done to you – just "fore-give" -- give forth. Release, let it drift away from you and don't carry that burden around.

Next, you address *ongoing* programming. Just because you're over the age of six doesn't mean you're immune to the constant bombardment of (mis)information that keeps you stuck. Along this line, if I could put this one in big, flashing letters, I would: please do NOT fall asleep in front of the TV! You have no idea how much convincing of your big, beautiful subconscious is going on. Convincing you that you're sick, depressed, losing your libido, losing your looks and aging so quickly that you need "their" products is what TV and to a lesser extent radio ads are doing all the time, especially if you're not paying close attention.

And if you're drifting off or fully asleep? Your subconscious is wide open, absorbing like a sponge. When you're asleep, your conscious mind (the filter that weighs what makes sense) is switched off, taking a much-needed break, and the vulnerable, wide-open mind of the child is all ears and ready to be convinced. If you have any doubts, do a web search on sleep-teaching and see how effective it's been shown to be. People learn whole foreign languages that way!

And while we're at it, keep in mind that even when you're awake, those ads are repeating. Remember what we said about repetition and how it changes neural pathways? This is no accident. Ads repeat for a reason, and it is specifically to plant ideas in your head so you'll act on them. As a trainer, I have seen the astonishing power of repetition time and again in my classroom, and again, awareness is power. Stop and consider: what's being sold to you so often you don't even notice you're coming to believe it?

Ongoing programming is also happening when you're around people who are complaining about getting older, you half-see the print ads in magazines that tout "anti-aging" products, and you yourself may automatically repeat the aging party line because it's gotten so deeply ingrained it seems natural. Again, it's so much easier to go along with the (hypnotized, not really choosing) crowd than to say, "no, stop – this doesn't feel good and I have decided I won't own it". You're ready to do something different, I hope, and as you've figured out, thoughts and feelings are the first things that have to change.

The scripts, visualizations and daily affirmations – whatever forms you find *feel* the best to you – will be the most effective. Again, you're overwriting old programming that's not going to get you what you want, and you have to be vigilant about not absorbing more ongoing messages that would just reinforce it. Go by how you feel. Change your train of thought if it feels nasty, because the effect it's having on your body is exactly that.

Along the path though, the physical things you can do, like eating right and getting regular exercise, will support you. Could you change your mind and not bother with the cool new healthier foods and working up a sweat on a regular basis? Maybe – but I for one am taking no chances. I don't want to do this half way – I want to eliminate as many speed bumps as possible and I know that part of my own belief set – my paradigm – is that optimal nutrition and movement are foundational to rejuvenation. And speaking of speed, recognize one thing – transformation has a gestation period like any other process.

If you put a seed in fertile soil and make sure it gets sunlight and water, you're not going to go out a few days later and dig it up to see if it's sprouting. You know you need to give it its own time – according to its own wisdom – to sprout and flourish. The same thing applies here. Depending on how deeply ingrained your old beliefs and habits are, it could take a while to overwrite and reinvent them; while for someone who tends to be optimistic and is ready to do the work of noticing, identifying the opposite of what's not wanted and scripting, visualizing, doing the physical steps and *enjoying the process* I'd be really surprised if 90 days went by without noticeable changes taking place in not only how you look and feel, but how well the rest of your life seems to fall into that improved place as well.

This is like-attracts-like, and if you are starting to avoid things or people that bring you down, or at least be aware and try not to let yourself get dragged down, you're going to find it easier and easier to dwell on things that make you feel good. The healthier eating, exercise, periods of quiet meditation where you still the "monkey mind" and let the wisdom in the Infinite impress itself upon you, all serve to make you less vulnerable to the occasional slings and arrows. Even those off times serve to show you what you don't want (from which, of course, you derive what you *do* want, and give that your focus.) You will likely find that strokes of creativity well up from within you, and your interest in things that further enrich your life experience become important to you.

CHAPTER 9

The Quantum Connection

I sing the body electric

The armies of those I love engirth me, and I engirth them....

- Walt Whitman -

Why? Why does what's on the inside become what's on the outside? And how? The why is unknown and even the how isn't entirely clear; but as I mentioned very early on, science and spirituality are coming to a lot of the same conclusions and it's a bit unexpected for them both. The theologian tells us that God, by any name, created everything. The scientist tells us that the energy field of pure potential is all around us and can be touched and shaped – what's called "collapsing the wave" into physical form. What if they're both right?

What if pure energy, organized by Consciousness, has created everything we see (and don't) and has blessed us with the ability to shape our lives from that infinite field of possibility? What if we're collaborating with that Consciousness – what some scientists are coming to call the Mind of God - in every moment? What if we're not passive bystanders but actually co-creating everything in our lives?

What if, when you stare off toward a wall, not particularly focused, you're looking not only through air that is invisible (well, unless you're in Los Angeles maybe), but through an invisible grid from which anything at all can be formed, and it's waiting for you to make a decision? What if that grid is this Consciousness and it is lovingly accommodating? There's an enormous body of research that points to exactly that, and whether you want to call it The Field, God, the Infinite Source, your own higher self that is loved by the Divine – it's up to you – it's not going away anytime soon, it's *always got its ears on*, and you'd better get familiar with it and do the work to shape the potential in a good way, or you will create by default, truly putting yourself in the position of reinforcing every negative reaction. Do you imagine your old programming, giving off messages about defeat, sickness of mind and body and eventual decay because of the passage of experience called aging, is working on shaping anything good?

Among the things we do know for certain is that our thoughts give off energy – vibration, if you will, with varying frequencies. If they didn't, brainwaves couldn't be measured and certain emotions wouldn't cause certain regions of the brain to "light up." We also know (again, for certain) that various ranges of brainwave frequency are associated with different states of mind, such as the alert but relaxed state in which people learn best, and that others correspond to sleeping, meditating, or hypnosis. More recent discoveries by ingenious folks like the ones at Heartmath in California, tell us that the human heart gives off an amazing amount of energy as well -- way more than the brain, by the way – and that it is affected by thought and emotion.

The entire disciplines of acupuncture, acupressure, deep tissue massage and color therapy depend upon the reliability and *predictability* of energy patterns in the human body, and it's not confined inside our skin, or the instruments that measure it from the outside wouldn't have anything to measure. So, okay – what this amounts to is that we're all walking, talking energy-broadcasting and -receiving organisms.

Have doubts about the receiving part? Walk into a tense business meeting or a funeral home where someone beloved by many is being eulogized. Listen to a radio station when a political pundit is angrily pouring out vitriol and see how you feel after five or ten minutes of it. Stand in a crowded room for a while and note that if you feel as though someone's eyes are on you, a quick scan of the room will find the face focused on you. Phrases like "the atmosphere was so thick you could cut it with a knife" didn't come about because it was a foggy day in Des Moines – they're based on a very human recognition that we pick up on other people's vibes and they pick up ours.

So what's all that energy doing? Is it just radiating out from each of us, like beams of light from a light bulb, with nothing happening as a result? Do the beams of light from the sun radiate out without effect? Make no mistake – each and every one of us, in every moment of every day is radiating energy, and depending upon whether we've allowed ourselves to remain in the gerbil wheel of unconscious habit, or decided to take thought and action toward a better existence, we will either poke along in some kind of assumed helplessness or live an astonishing life. We are touching that field of infinite possibilities – that grid from which everything is created – with the energy we give off, whether we're aware of it or not, and we do have a choice of what to make for ourselves with it.

That's a huge responsibility, but without acknowledging it and deciding to make it work in our favor, we allow random vibes from any- and everywhere to shape what *we then live*. Think about that – do you want the people around you who are always broke, always unhappy, always complaining, always behind the 8-ball shaping how *your* life plays out? If you don't get a handle on the fact that even their proximity, much less conversation puts you in a bad frame of mind and *do* something about it, you get pulled along by it. You'll be sucked into the same stream as theirs that's trickling downhill, others who are that way too will find you comforting, the stream becomes a raging river, and to put it bluntly, you're screwed. Is that what you want?!

A lot has been written about what's called The Law of Attraction, and whether you brush it off as so much New-Age stuff that you don't "believe" or come to recognize that it's really nothing more than quantum physics at work in a pretty predictable way, it bears consideration. The scenario above could be entirely different, depending on whether you decide to decide. Decide what you do with the vibes you're willing to accept *and the kind you decide to put out there.* Consciousness and the field from which you form your life aren't going away – ignoring them doesn't turn them off.

You may as well consciously decide and do something with them that you can live with and love.

CHAPTER 10

The Single Greatest Thing

There is a final piece to this personal puzzle, and it is a transformative tool that is talked about a lot and practiced far too little – a tool I believe to be the crowning glory of thought-feeling-spirit integration. It is gratitude. How much do we actually practice being grateful? I know I didn't – at least not very much – during a good deal of my young adult years. There was always something I could point to that wasn't working, didn't seem fair, didn't feel good; and when I was surprised by a favorable outcome, I was excited for all of a day or so before slipping right back into that rut of focusing on what I didn't like, didn't want – you know how that goes. If you had asked me then what I was grateful for, I would've probably stared wide-eyed and mute -- as my friend Tracy says, "….crickets." No sound coming out. No idea what I could possibly be grateful for.

A lot has changed for me, and it hasn't been just that my outer circumstances have changed – it's been an inner change. Not that I don't focus on what's unlikable in my life at times – I haven't evolved to where I never let anything get to me – but I've discovered that even when things happen that really stink, there's usually a way I can *reframe* whatever it is; and when I do, I can usually find something in there that's worthy of my gratitude. Sometimes I can do it pretty quickly, like a recent morning when I was supposed to be downtown for an appointment and hadn't left myself quite enough time for the drive.

I was grumbling and annoyed with myself when it struck me that it could just be that I would be benefitted somehow by being late. I pulled over, got out my cell and called to say I'd be a bit late and was told "thanks – no problem." I sat for a moment, sure that this was for a reason, thanking All That Is for whatever it was that I was being spared by being delayed. About eight or nine miles further along the road, I drove by what looked to be a minor accident, and some civilians were directing traffic around it, as the police had not yet arrived. There was my answer. That's what I wasn't supposed to be part of.

At other times, it's been something big and very personal that has happened, and it seems that the moment I can turn away from the hurt, fear or anger and find my way back to recognizing I'm being provided for somehow – whether I see it immediately or not – and I can be grateful for whatever good there is in it, I'm blessed with what I need. That can be awfully hard to do, especially if something that feels truly threatening is right up in my face; but this is one of those areas where practice makes it easier and easier. I'm a work in progress like everyone else.

Some years ago, I wrote a series of articles for a country living e-zine, and the title of the series was A Year of Living Thoughtfully. I had been on my own for a while, starting over on a modest salary, so the focus of the articles was the relearning of some important skills like basic frugality and living simply. I had done one article on the construction of window quilts, and gotten some lovely feedback. This is an excerpt from the article that then followed.

Journal Entry, February 9th

Energy savings aside, I've been enjoying spending nights with my sewing. The garage/wood shop is too cold to work in this year (a heater-and-dust-collection fund has its own sock now where a few dollar bills get tucked away - maybe next year) so it feels good to spend at least an hour or two practicing long-neglected sewing skills, knowing that one by one, each window of my house will eventually have color and warmth. This brings me to the last thought I want to leave you with -- gratitude. Do you remember the article I wrote called The Notebook? It has taken on a new dimension.*

I was sitting down to pay bills and work out this month's budget recently, doing my best to fight back the gnawing fears.... I had done a first pass at my taxes and was astounded to find that after refinancing the house and all that it took during '08, my income literally fell below the poverty level. But it didn't feel that way. It felt blessed and imbued with a quiet fullness. I looked around me and decided to approach my list of places that my salary would need to go in a different way. Instead of a list down the left side of the page with a corresponding dollar amount at the far right, I decided to write what each of those things represented to me.

<u>Mortgage</u>   *My haven, my home, a stout structure of my own design -- the land around me resplendent with every kind of animal and plant, of which I am entrusted with sacred stewardship. Thank you.*

<u>*Taxes & Insurance*</u>   *Security - knowing I can weather the storms - supporting the education of children*

> *who may some day run this country, libraries,*
> *roadways, help for the helpless. Thank you.*

Propane   *Blessed warmth on the coldest nights; the luxury of hot*
              water to bathe with and keep my home clean. Thank you.

*On and on I went, writing faster and faster with each category until I
had to stop because my eyes were overflowing and I could no longer see
the paper under my pen.*

*The power of that exercise made it possible for me to go to work
shortly afterward and approach my boss - a man charged with an
enormous amount of responsibility amid sliding morale. I asked him
what he'd think of turning an entire wall in the hallway of our building
a Gratitude Wall. To my delight and surprise, he threw his support
behind it; and as I write, the first dozen messages have already reached
a sort of "in-box" on my cubicle wall and my email box. Some are
personal. Some professional. All are genuine.*

> *"I'm so relieved my father-in-law is feeling better."*

> *"Thanks, Millie, for your help and support."*

> *"I'm grateful to be working with such a wonderful
> group of people...."*

*As I gather each few messages, I format them, give each a different
typeface and border, and put them up on a newly mounted collection
of cork bulletin boards purchased specifically for the Gratitude Wall.
There has been no bit of resentment at money being spent for the sake*

of uplifting the spirits of both those who express their positive sentiments and those who pause to take in those precious good wishes.

To paraphrase a well-worn commercial, "...good feelings shared - priceless."

*The notebook I had written an article about was a little black journal I carry in my purse – I mentioned it a few chapters back. I have glued pictures on a few of the pages of a puppy who looks a lot like my dog Barney did when he was little, and whenever something nice happens – someone gives me a compliment, I get a rebate in the mail, the people in my classes tell me on the evaluation forms how much they feel they got out of it – anything at all that I know is a blessing small or large - I write down. Not only does it help me notice and focus on all the good coming my way, but on those occasions when there's a bit too much of what the Abraham-Hicks folks call "contrast" (i.e. the stuff that sucks) I can take that journal out, read back through the pages and look at the pictures and I am reminded once again that sure, some things aren't working; but I have to admit, a whole lot more is, and I am grateful beyond measure.

One of the exercises I like to have people do, especially if they tend to be kind of glum and pessimistic and would rather go off on tangents about how awful this in the news or that going on in politics is, is start brainstorming about things that we're all grateful for. Most people start with the obvious things like gratitude that they have their health, or their families, or their jobs – even if it's one they're not crazy about (haven't we all been there?) but before long, you can see how they're opening up and looking at so much that they normally look past and totally take for granted. And you know what? Sometimes they have the same reaction I did to my budget! Stop and think about it for a second.

Aren't you glad somebody built all the roads and bridges that make it possible for you to drive around? And what about things like window glass that lets in the light but not the wind? What about the food on your table? If you have a dog, aren't you glad there's a tail wagging behind the door when you get home? Isn't it amazing to realize that even if you're not happy right now with the shape your body's in, you can change it? Aren't all of those, things you can be grateful for? I believe that there is truly no greater frequency of energy you can give to those around you and to the grid of potential than the depth of love that gratitude exemplifies.

In parting, I would like to say that one of the tenets of quantum physics that is both mind-boggling and thought-provoking is the property of interconnectedness. The theory is that everyone and everything – all created at the time of the Big Bang – are somehow still interconnected. If we consider for a moment that the grid is invisible to us but that the potential for all existence arises from it, it's not that hard to conceptualize an unbroken continuum from which all arises and all returns.

Scientists prove it by taking two particles and separating them by considerable distance and then observing that when something affects one particle, the other reacts instantaneously. Mind you, Spinoza didn't know anything about particles and waves during the 1600s, but he did sense that unity was at the bottom of all existence (and he did a dandy job of alienating Des Cartes, who was all about separating the observed from the observer) but I digress.

People from all ages, even without the exactitude of quantum mechanical experiments that produce the same results over and over, were keen observers and they've been saying the same thing, each in their different time/place languages. We are all part of a connected One.

Consider, then, that what we put out on the grid – what we touch it with and form from it – as well as all those beams of energy we're putting out that touch and affect those around us, are under our control. We can choose – quite a bit more consciously now, once we've become aware and learned to work with the giant part of our minds – what to practice putting out there and expecting in return. Like attracts like. What goes around comes around. Karma.

Call it what you will, but recognize that you do have a choice in every waking moment what to focus on and bring into your life; and if you choose well, you not only shape an amazing existence for yourself, but you contribute to the health and happiness of everyone else. And yes, it comes back to you multiplied. The flap of the butterfly's wings isn't the only thing affecting the world.

Remember the principle of new assumptions – the way a mass belief or paradigm is changed. All it's going to take is one person or perhaps a few for reinforcement who will shine like beacons, for everyone else to know they can do something too. If what you want is to free yourself and those you care about of the old paradigm around aging – if you're actually ready to change your mind and change your life, you have all the tools. You need only willingness to start and the commitment to persist. I wish you both.

-S. Ellesson

April 2014

REFERENCES AND RECOMMENDED READING

The reading list that follows is extremely informal, though I'm sure these books can be found by title and author thanks to the power of the 'net. Some are quite old, some relatively new – all have value. In no order other than grouped by category and the way they were lined up in my bookcases, the following were some of the sources of information that went into this book, and will provide anyone who wants to dig deeper with plenty of foundational knowledge (not to mention, a lot of them are just good reads!)

The first group are some **books that approach the mind/ emotion/energy** subject from a number of different perspectives:

Excuse Me, Your Life is Waiting by Lynn Grabhorn

Ask and It Is Given by Esther and Jerry Hicks

The Master Key System by Charles F. Haanel

The Biology of Belief by Bruce H. Lipton, PhD

The Spontaneous Healing of Belief by Gregg Braden

The Secret by Rhonda Byrne

Invisible Acts of Power by Caroline Myss

Feeling is the Secret by Neville Goddard

The Formula by Vernon M. Sylvest, M.D.

The Nature of Personal Reality by Jane Roberts

The Holotropic Mind by Stanislav Grof, M.D.

Thought Forces Essays by Prentice Mulford

Real Magic by Wayne W. Dyer

Spontaneous Evolution by Bruce H. Lipton, PhD and Steve Bhaerman

The next group of books are, again, different approaches to **healthy eating**:

Healthful Cuisine by Anna Maria Clement, PhD and Chef Kelly Serbonich

The Eat-Clean Diet by Tosca Reno

Staying Healthy With the Seasons by Elson M. Haas, M.D.

Healing With Whole Foods by Paul Pitchford

The Dynamics of Nutrition by Gerhard Schmidt

Perfect Health by Deepak Chopra, M.D.

Master your Metabolism by Jillian Michaels

The last group is on **quantum physics, spirituality and creation** and again, as with the categories above, is only a small sampling of what's available. Look for book reviews and discussions on my website healthnutliving.com

God & The New Physics by Paul Davies

The Laws of Manifestation by David Spangler

The Self-Aware Universe by Amit Goswami, PhD

Wholeness and the Implicate Order by David Bohm

Conscious Acts of Creation By Wm Tiller, PhD, Walter Dibble Jr PhD and Michael Kohane, PhD

Quantum Physics and Theology – An Unexpected Kinship by John Polkinghorne

Who's Afraid of Schrodinger's Cat by Ian Marshal and Danah Zohar w/ F. David Peat